COLLABORATIVE ACTION FOR EQUITY AND OPPORTUNITY

COLLABORATIVE ACTION FOR EQUITY AND OPPORTUNITY

A Practical Guide for School and Community Leaders

PAUL REVILLE
LYNNE SACKS

HARVARD EDUCATION PRESS
CAMBRIDGE, MASSACHUSETTS

Paperback ISBN 978-1-68253-595-0
Library Edition ISBN 978-1-68253-596-7

Library of Congress Cataloging-in-Publication data is on file.

Published by Harvard Education Press,
an imprint of the Harvard Education Publishing Group

Harvard Education Press
8 Story Street
Cambridge, MA 02138

Cover Design: Ciano Design
Cover Photo: <<to come>>

The typefaces used in this book are Sabon and ITC Legacy Sans.

Contents

Preface

Collaborative Action for Children: The Urgency of Now

The first time it hit me was when I was acting as a judge in a city school system science fair. Armed with our clipboards, we judges dutifully made our way up and down long rows of little booths, each featuring eager students anxious to tell us about their projects. We listened closely, asked probing questions, and then carefully marked our scorecards, rating the substance of each project and the skills of the student presenter.

When I had finished a couple of hours of this demanding job, two students stuck out in my mind. The first, I'll call him James, came from one of the city's highest-achieving and most affluent schools. He did a project on neuroscience, literally on brain surgery. His project was festooned with scientific and medical artifacts. He had a model of a brain, surgical tools, complex illustrations, and colorful diagrams attractively arrayed on a pair of large folding panels. His knowledge was deep and impressive, well beyond what we'd expect of a fifth grader. In the course of our conversation, he revealed that his father was a physician in the neuroscience department at the medical school in town. His father had been eager and generous in helping him with his project.

A little farther down the same row was another talented student. Adrianna, a recent immigrant attending one of the city's poorest schools, had done a project on photosynthesis. She was shy and spoke in halting English about how she had gone to the public library on her own, found some books on photosynthesis, copied some of the pages on the library's copier, and pasted them to the rumpled poster board she'd purchased at CVS. She was clearly bright, had loads of initiative, and was very enthusiastic about her topic, but her knowledge of photosynthesis appeared limited. She had received no parental assistance whatsoever in assembling her project.

At the end of the day, I was called upon to objectively rate these two students, and many others, on the quality of their projects and presentations. On the basis of the criteria on my judging score sheet, there was absolutely no question that James's project was superior and likely the winner, while Adrianna's was at or toward the bottom of the pack. But what was I really rating? Their own skill and knowledge or their parents' social and economic capital and ability to advance their children's academic careers? Here were two students only in fifth grade, and the advantages one enjoyed outside of school relative to the other appeared already to have determined their life prospects, regardless of anything that might happen in school.

In the future, James would benefit from extraordinary supports and opportunities at every stage of his education. He would enjoy stable, comfortable housing; comprehensive health care; excellent nutrition; safety; and security. In the 80 percent of his waking hours spent outside of school, James would be showered with stimulating, enriching opportunities ranging from afterschool programs to summer camps, tutoring, travel, access to learning technologies, SAT prep, specialized sports training, and much, much more. His life out of school would be a veritable buffet of enrichment intentionally designed by his parents to provide him with maximum advantage in the competition for elite college admission and high-paying, prestigious employment. Should he experience adversity along the way, his family would provide a network of connections and resources to aid him in overcoming his challenges. With such help, he would, in all probability, not only achieve at high levels in school and extracurricular activities but ultimately be very successful in college and his career.

By contrast, Adrianna, through no fault of her own, would very likely face a legion of obstacles to her success, obstacles common to children with her social-economic status. Her family could be forced to move regularly to find safe, affordable housing. She would likely be the victim of anti-immigrant and ethnic discrimination and would also be likely to experience a number of childhood traumas, including witnessing violence in her neighborhood. She would get her health care from the emergency room when she desperately needed it but wouldn't receive basics like dental care. Her diet would feature a lot of processed foods because her neighborhood is a food desert. The water she drinks may be unsafe, and the air she breathes polluted. Adrianna is every bit as capable in the abstract as James, but her circumstances conspire against her. She won't have much access to enrichment opportunities outside of school, in the afternoons, on weekends, and in the summer, because her mother has to work two jobs just to make ends meet. She will be obligated to miss school fairly often to take care of younger siblings because of the high cost of daycare. She'll have a nearly impossible time competing with the likes of James. In due course, she may get discouraged, drop out, and go to work in a low-paying job just so she can provide the family with some income. Through no fault of her own, or lack of talent or grit, Adrianna's college and career prospects are not bright.

What is clear is that these two children of comparable aptitude and cultural endowments will be profoundly advantaged or disadvantaged by their life's circumstances, by the existence of poverty and discrimination. Their odds of being successful are widely different, and on average, schooling is simply too weak an intervention to overcome these odds. We've always had inequality in America. There is evidence that these problems are worsening and urgently need interrogation and remedy. Nonetheless, Americans, in spite of much evidence to the contrary, have long sustained a belief that our country is a meritocracy, an equal opportunity society. And what makes it a society where anyone's talent and effort can propel them to the top? Our public education system. The school system is supposed to lift everyone up to a "level playing field," give everyone a fair chance to succeed in spite of pervasive inequality. Horace Mann, the founder of modern public education, said it best and first: "[E]ducation above all else is the great balance wheel of society." But more than a century and a half from Mann's time, the balance wheel effect hasn't materialized. School systems have tried their best to perform the balance wheel function but with limited success, even when they strive to provide equal treatment for all students—which is rare because, unfortunately, much of our school history has been characterized by unequal, unfair treatment of the most disadvantaged students, compounding the adverse circumstances of their lives and making it impossible for all but a relative few to defy the odds.

This book addresses the question of what we do if the whole premise of public schools as the great equalizer is flawed. The data indicate that this is exactly the case. Despite individual examples to the contrary, the institution of public K–12 schooling, which occupies only 20 percent of a student's waking hours between ages five and eighteen, is, on average, not nearly a strong enough treatment to create an equal opportunity society. If we accept this as true (and if you doubt it, look at the persistent, strong correlation between educational opportunity, achievement, and attainment with socioeconomic status), what do we do?[1] Americans have been struggling with this question since the authors of the "Nation at Risk" report sounded a clarion call that our public education system was, in 1983, woefully outdated, outmoded, and uncompetitive. The report's rhetoric was powerful and urgent: "If an unfriendly foreign power had attempted to impose on America the mediocre educational performance that exists today, we might well have viewed it as an act of war" and "the educational foundations of our society are presently being eroded by a *rising tide of mediocrity*." The authors of this report and many others at that time called for a transformation in US schooling. We might well do the same again today, because we are still a nation at risk.

A few years after the jarring "Nation at Risk" report, the nation's governors and business leaders met at President George H. W. Bush's Education Summit in Charlottesville, Virginia, and pledged to do whatever was needed to fix the schools so that they might deliver on Mann's ideal. They did so because they saw our system of schooling as a human capital development system, but one that was badly flawed, incapable of preparing this nation's youth, and thus our society and economy, to compete effectively in the twenty-first century.

In response to "Nation at Risk" and other calls for change, "fix the schools" became the mantra. The theory of action was, and in many quarters continues to be, that US schools were failing to achieve Mann's ideal simply because they were inefficient and ineffective. The belief in the myth that schooling can yield a meritocracy in spite of pervasive inequality was durable. Proponents of various ideological stripes insisted that the schools were subpar for a variety of different reasons. One school of thought was that schools were intentionally designed to reproduce the existing social order. Failure was deliberately built into the model. More mainstream critics believed that schools simply weren't managed well, were too unionized, while still others pointed to educators being not sufficiently savvy about teaching and learning, while still others blamed poor performance on inadequate school funding. If we could fix these problems, school optimization advocates (and full disclosure, I was certainly one) argued, we would transform the schools to the point where they would become the instruments of equity that Mann had envisioned. Schools would finally become the great equalizers.

States, starting with Kentucky, launched the now nearly three-decades-old era of standards-based reform, a massive initiative, backed by business leaders, governors, the federal government, major philanthropies, state governments, and ultimately, local school systems. The origin of this movement was an economic imperative—build a human capital system to drive the growth of a twenty-first-century, high-skills, high-knowledge economy. In a felicitous coincidence, the interests of big business converged with the interests of equity advocates. There was widespread embrace of the belief that the nation needed a system to educate all (and "all means all," as Kentucky reformers asserted) children to high levels of skill and knowledge so that they could successfully participate in a twenty-first-economy that was rapidly shedding its low-skill, low-knowledge jobs.

This was a radical reform, a dramatic revision in policy makers' expectations for US public education. A system that heretofore had only educated a few elite students to top levels was now being charged with and held accountable for educating all children to top, world-class levels. The school reform movement was powerful and sweeping, ultimately embracing all the states and becoming the official policy of the United States government. It was incredibly ambitious. It had widespread support. It was a movement driven by competitive economic pressure and ideals of excellence and equity, coupled with a yearning for continuous improvement. The strategies employed such as standards, assessments, accountability, data use, focus on teaching, choice, and turning around chronically underperforming schools were all commonsense approaches utilized in various other sectors. In the end, however, these strategies proved necessary but not sufficient to achieve the goals of education reform.

In my home state, Massachusetts, I was lucky enough to be able to play a role in this movement, first as head of a local education fund, then as cofounder of the Massachusetts Business Alliance for Education (where I had a role in creating the historic Education Reform Act of 1993), then as a member of the state board of education (on two separate occasions for two different governors from different political parties), next as chairman of the state board of education, and finally as secretary of education for the Commonwealth of Massachusetts. In all of these roles and others, I had an impact on the policy and practice of reform in a state that became known for the strength of its school reform work.

Massachusetts enacted education reform more effectively than most other places, and the results showed and were celebrated far and wide. I was proud of our carefully crafted reforms. As a reform leader, I celebrated our comparative success, not only in leading the nation but in arriving at or near the top of the world on some achievement measures. However, I was painfully aware that while we celebrated literally decades of first-place National Assessment of Educational Progress (NAEP) finishes, we have some of the widest achievement gaps in the nation. All of our high rankings are based on achievement scores, calculated by averaging, thereby concealing the fact that we still have hundreds of thousands of youth being under- or mis-educated, totally unprepared for success. Our gaps between various subgroups were and continue to be larger than comparable gaps in most other states. And we had set out to achieve "all means all"! By this standard, I realized, we'd have to view our education reform efforts as a failure. And the results, nationally, were no better.

In fact, nationally, the results were even worse. After a quarter century of education reform, we, as a nation, have merely made modest progress in raising student achievement, closing gaps, and preparing our young people for success. We have come nowhere close to putting all of our children on an equal footing or preparing all of them to participate effectively in today's economy. We have left millions of children behind because we have not provided anywhere near all of them with the skills, knowledge, and disposition to be successful as workers in a twenty-first-century, high-skills, high-knowledge economy, as citizens in a complex democracy, family heads, and lifelong learners.

When education reform was all said and done, we still had a nearly iron-law correlation between socioeconomic status and educational achievement and attainment.

Where did we go wrong?

We tinkered with schooling but made no changes to the basic design and fundamental premises behind our school system. We tinkered with the legacy school system, accepting its factory-model structure and norms, its one-size-fits-all pedagogy, its peculiarly outdated calendar and schedule, its monopolistic bureaucracy, and its avoidance of attention to the impact of poverty, racism, and the myriad factors affecting if and how children show up at school. What David Tyack and Larry Cuban called the "grammar of schooling" remained intact and ultimately proved, even in the face of massive and expensive reform efforts, to be unequal to the challenges of the twenty-first-century.[2] We had set massively ambitious policy goals of educating all children to internationally benchmarked standards of skill and knowledge, and yet we had failed to change the fundamental system of schooling that had been designed for another purpose in another era.

I used to begin my Education Reform class at Harvard with an unvarnished look at the underlying theory of action behind the school reform movement. I'd start with a profile of two students: one, my youngest daughter, and the other a hypothetical classmate of hers from the same urban public school system. I'd paint a picture of inequality similar to the one illustrated by the lives of James and Adrianna. The inequalities afflicting the Adriannas of this world begin early, go deep, and persist. In class, I'd describe how my daughter, Addy, started kindergarten with two parents, having heard millions more words than many of her classmates, having been read to in English nightly, having already traveled all over the world, having had quality day care, great nutrition, and total stability and safety, while her classmate Marcus had none of that and quite likely many traumatic events with which to cope. The school system was supposed to erase these differences in advantage and disadvantage, but it was failing to do that because it was never designed for that purpose. School reform would have to fix the system to achieve the recently recognized imperative to educate all students to the level heretofore reserved for the elite few. That was a tall order.

Despite the fact that Marcus has the same aptitude as Addy and his parents have high aspirations for him, the probability that he will enjoy academic and career success and a middle-class life are far below those of Addy. He may well overcome these odds, but the data suggest he has a very steep hill to climb.

I knew this from my own experience as a child of privilege. I came from a comfortable, not wealthy, upper-middle-class family. Through the accident of birth, I inherited access to the opportunities and supports that have enabled me to be relatively successful. When, in college, I came to the realization that I'd landed on third base not because I'd hit a triple but because I'd been lucky, I dedicated my career to equity and education.

But it took me decades of work in the field to understand, viscerally and not just intellectually, that fixing a deeply flawed school system requires not only attacking the most obvious markers of racism, inequitable funding, and segregation, not only strengthening the transactions, called teaching and learning, that transpire between teachers, curricula, and students but dismantling the basic, factory architecture of our one-size-fits-all school system that was designed to, at best, provide the same treatment to everybody and thereby reproduce the existing social order.

As I returned to Harvard after my tenure as secretary, with equal measures of pride and disappointment in Massachusetts' educational performance, I realized all too well that our reforms of schooling had been necessary but not sufficient to fundamentally change student outcomes. I had a strong conviction that schools alone, as currently constituted, could not achieve the policy goal of "all means all." I was convinced that we needed to re-envision our education system and conceive of a broader child development and education system that would genuinely be designed to achieve the purpose of preparing all students for success. We could no longer tinker with our early-twentieth-century Model T, our factory-based system of schooling, because its design was based on the early-twentieth-century need to prepare only the small number of students, roughly 10 percent, to do the high-knowledge jobs, leaving 90 percent ready for routine factory work.

I realized that if we were to deliver on the rhetorical promise of all means all, we would have to redesign our entire approach to preparing young people to become adults. While we knew what wasn't working and for whom in our current system, we were still unclear on what would work more effectively. How would we redesign education systems to achieve our ambitious policy goals calling for a high standard of achievement for all? What would be the design principles? What would the architecture look like? I was convinced that we needed an education redesign lab to lead a process to answer these and other questions, to change the national conversation on education to something broader and bolder. The experience of that lab forms the basis for the work described in this book.

At the heart of our work would be a challenge to the underlying design principle of our current system: that fairness is achieved by giving everyone the same treatment. While that sounds logical, equity (fairness) and equality (the same for everyone) are not always identical. An equitable system would give everyone what they need to achieve a uniformly high standard of achievement. If everyone gets what they need, then all children, and all means all, have a genuine opportunity to achieve success. Children's needs differ, so not everyone will receive the same curriculum, instruction, services, and supports from school. Their educational programs will need to vary to reflect their particular needs.

Imagine a child arriving in the United States from Syria. Her father had been a doctor, but the ongoing violence had cost his job and interrupted her education. Just getting to the United States has taken great resilience, but she's placed in a grade commensurate with her age despite speaking no English and missing foundational subjects. She will have a very different set of needs than her classmate, a privileged child of affluent parents who has enjoyed a lifetime of advantages that allow him to easily move forward in the dominant culture. Our school system should prepare both of these children for success, but that can't happen if we treat them both the same. We wouldn't do that in a hospital: give everyone, irrespective of their ailment, the same treatment because we thought that was fair or because it was just easier for us as adults to do the same thing for everyone. No. We'd diagnose each incoming patient and then prescribe what would be needed to get that patient to the standard of health. So, in schooling, we should meet children where they are and give them what they need to be successful. To be explicit, the girl from Syria will need different forms of instruction and more instructional time to meet her learning goals. We need to create an education system that can be responsive and customized to meet individual needs like hers.

Of course, this is much easier said than done. Building systems of opportunity and support to meet children where they are and give them what they need is indeed a monumental challenge, and the school reform movement was unable to do that. We have yet to see any community build, at scale, a cradle-to-career, longitudinal, education and child development pipeline that ensures the success of all children. The core of that pipeline needs to be an integrated, formal education system that includes preschool, kindergarten, through grade 12 and postsecondary education, leading to a job. Wrapped around that pipeline needs to be a rich insulating fabric of opportunities and supports, comparable to those enjoyed by affluent families. Such resources, supports, and opportunities must be available to all children because they matter in preparing young people to be successful. For those who don't have access to such services and opportunities via the accident of birth, we must create public systems that provide comparable services, thus leveling the playing field with respect to opportunity to succeed.

This twenty-first-century design work, building a child development and education system that meets the needs of individuals and society, is, I am convinced, the most important work of our times. This book aims to present some mechanisms and tools for doing this complex work collaboratively, in ways that work for all concerned. In the end, this is how we will get to a prosperous future and the ideal of "all means all."

—*Paul Reville*

Introduction

This book and our work at the Education Redesign Lab (EdRedesign) are dedicated to the creation of a new system of education and child development, led by local Children's Cabinets and built to meet the lofty goals policy makers have rather casually imposed on today's educators. We must concede that schools alone, even if optimized, are insufficient for building an equal opportunity society, let alone a uniformly high-skill, high-knowledge workforce. Children who grow up in poverty, whether in rural, urban, or suburban areas, are often the victims of racism, economic marginalization, and toxic stress born of adverse experiences. If we want them to have the same kinds of educational outcomes and college and career success enjoyed by their more affluent peers, then they must have access to the same array of supports and opportunities that enable more privileged children to come to school every day ready to learn. Such supports and opportunities are routinely afforded to affluent youngsters and enable these children to build resilience and increase learning in ways that provide them a clear advantage. If we truly want to "leave no child behind," if we are genuinely strategizing to have every student succeed, then we need a system that does for all children what those who have privilege do for their own. This is a system that looks very different from what we have today. This is a system built to achieve social, racial, and economic justice. It's a system built to achieve America's aspirational but unrealized goals for education: excellence and equity.

This book presents the concept and design of such a system, a handbook for local policy makers, community leaders, and educators who seek a child development and education system designed to prepare each and every child to be successful in work, citizenship, family, and community life. In these pages, we articulate a vision, its rationale, and the ways and means that change leaders in various communities have employed to build a "broader, bolder" approach to child development in education. We seek to describe for practitioners the why, what, and how of such a system. We aim to provide the tools, strategies, and a road map to creating new mechanisms in communities to more effectively nurture and develop their children.

At no time in our history has such a transformation of our education system been needed more than in the present. Besieged by a worldwide pandemic, awakened by uprisings demanding long overdue racial and social justice, and confronted with the widespread failure of education reform to close persistent educational achievement and attainment gaps, we must find a way to do better by our children, or our society, economy, and democracy will crumble. The economic and democratic health of our communities, our prosperity, depends on this work of readying all of our children to successfully meet the challenges of the twenty-first century. We are failing to do that now, and our failure has left us "a nation at risk" more than ever before.

In this historical moment, we have both great danger and opportunity due to the pandemic. The dangers to our health, economy, and society are obvious to most people, but the opportunities should not be overlooked. For example, widespread school closings due to the pandemic exposed many in the general public, for the first time, to the realities of the underclass in our country. Many people had blithely assumed that schools were dealing with the entire spectrum of children's needs, from nutrition to health care, personal safety, and things as mundane as internet connectivity. When the schools closed, it was as though a thick fog had been lifted revealing deep, disturbing inequities that were the lived experience for generations of Americans but had been only dimly, if at all, visible to the general public. Now, suddenly, the front pages of our media were filled with stories of schools struggling to bring food to families, to provide internet service, to get mental health supports to children. Yes, schools had always strived to help in each of these areas, but seldom did schools have the funding or staff capacity to meet the needs. The public's sudden awareness of and sympathy with those caught in these equity gaps present an opportunity for change. Children's Cabinets are well positioned to help coordinate emergency responses in a crisis like this, but even more importantly, Cabinets are ideally placed to seize such an opportunity for promoting lasting change in policies and budgets.

The Children's Cabinets detailed in this book are a mechanism for bringing together community leaders, "grass tops" as well as grassroots to focus on and collaborate to build more effective cradle-to-career pipelines for our children and youth. These pipelines consist of formal, universally accessible, high-quality systems of schooling: early education and care, kindergarten through high school systems, and postsecondary institutions of higher education. The formal systems are the piping. Wrapped around the pipe are insulating components of support and opportunity, elements of care, and enrichment that make it possible for children to thrive and take full advantage of their schooling. From the vantage point of children and their families, the components should be as seamless as the elaborate quilts of support and opportunity that middle- and upper-class families currently wrap around their own children. Families need accessible and affordable medical care and high-quality preschools for their young children. If their child has a developmental delay, they need to be able to have this assessed and get early intervention. As children reach school age, they should all have access to a high-quality education, with strong teachers, a rigorous curriculum, and high expectations. But they also need opportunities to explore and develop their interests and strengths through enrichment programs after school and during the summers. If they have experienced trauma or their family becomes homeless, social services should be readily available to mitigate the consequences.

The child's well-being must be of paramount importance. A child struggling academically should have access to individualized support targeted toward both her in- and out-of-school needs. As she moves through high school, she should have advising to help her decide on a postsecondary goal and apply to college or other programs that will help her achieve it. All these and other comparable supports need to be sustained over time, not just available for a year or two.

This is admittedly a tall and expensive order, which is why Children's Cabinets are not only designed for greater communication and collaboration for the purpose of delivering existing services to children, but even more importantly, to advocate for the policies and budget commitments that society must make in order to realize equal opportunity for our children. There are no cheap shortcuts or onetime inoculations that will free our society from making tough choices about how deeply we want to invest in developing our human capital, our children. Children's Cabinets force communities to confront critical choices about what needs to be done to promote children's well-being and success. The collaboration we urge is durable, sustainable, action-oriented engagement between civic, school, community, and youth leaders for purposes of prioritizing and meeting the needs of children.

The quest to build that comprehensive, cross-sector system of child support, development, and education is, in our view, the most important work of our times. If we succeed at building this system, one that is truly equitable, then our nation will prosper. If we fail to meet this challenge, our nation will suffer steep decline, a stagnant economy due to the lack of talent, and a growing underclass of people no longer able to find a foothold in the US economy and who will need to be financially supported by those who are able to find work. Not only do we have a moral responsibility to provide for those in the next generation and ensure that they have the best possible chance to develop their potential and lead happy, rewarding lives, but we have an economic imperative to preserve a prospering economy and a healthy, informed democracy.

Our experience tells us that the place to develop the comprehensive systems we will be describing is at the local level. We believe that with the countless distractions and deep divisiveness in our state and national political arenas, local leaders are best equipped to make common cause in solving persistent social problems. Because we live together and know one another in our local communities, we have a better shot at understanding, at assuming good faith even when our perspectives differ, and at engaging with political empathy in strategizing to solve handicapping conditions that constrain brighter possibilities for our people and our communities. At the local level, there's a higher probability that people can check their swords and shields at the door and come together around a Cabinet table to get something done in the community's interest. We're betting on local citizens and local leaders to be in the vanguard of this movement for children. As many examples in this book will describe, there is already a great deal of evidence that our faith in local communities is well justified.

Building this new system will take visionary leadership and committed, sustained effort over many years. At EdRedesign, we pledged to help create such a transformative system, not only by advocating for it, but by working directly with communities interested in constructing systems of child development and education that would work for all. Our work alongside these communities has enabled us to better understand what it takes to create and sustain meaningful new systems over an extended period of time. With this knowledge, we can distill and share important lessons with other cities and regions interested in undertaking this work.

To accomplish this, in 2016, EdRedesign formed a consortium of communities, called By All Means, to support cities and other jurisdictions interested in transforming the way they support children from birth through the successful completion of a postsecondary degree or credential. By design, these communities chose their own points of entry into the effort, although all shared several common features. These core elements included having a mayor and superintendent of schools committed to taking leadership roles in creating a comprehensive new system and to convening a Children's Cabinet to carry out the work.

Over the past four and a half years, EdRedesign has provided strategic guidance, twice-yearly meetings in service of a cohort-based approach to enable regular sharing of expertise and best practices, ongoing technical assistance, and part-time local support for ten By All Means communities. In 2018, we jointly created a second network, the Local Children's Cabinet Network, in collaboration with the Forum for Youth Investment and the Children's Funding Project, to support a broader set of thirty-five communities in designing cross-sector systems for children. A map of these communities is included in the appendix.

By All Means is grounded in the collective impact concept outlined by John Kania and Mark Kramer in their seminal article on this subject in the *Stanford Social Innovation Review* in 2011.[1] Our distinctive approach to this work entails an explicit focus on addressing the challenges of poverty while featuring the importance of mayoral or other top municipal leadership to spur action. Because of these distinctions, we call our approach "collaborative action."

EdRedesign is not the first organization to recognize the need to move beyond a solely school-based approach to changing trajectories for children. We join a group of organizations that have been working for years—and sometimes decades—to create place-based, comprehensive supports for children. These include Strive Together, the Forum for Youth Investment, Communities in Schools, PolicyLink, City Connects, the Harlem Children's Zone, Say Yes to Education, the Coalition for Community Schools, and others. These organizations each have somewhat different designs, but they all share the same overarching goal.

The number of communities participating in one or more of these cross-sector approaches is evidence that this is a set of ideas that resonates strongly with those who work with children. Since the publication of Kania and Kramer's article, hundreds of communities have undertaken collaborative action to benefit children and youth.[2] At EdRdesign, we see firsthand this interest in a new approach to education and child development, with cities regularly reaching out to us about their interest in being part of our approach to collaborative action on behalf of children.

Despite the strong resonance of this approach, creating new systems that translate to sustained improvements in opportunities and outcomes for children is difficult work beset by numerous barriers—financial, political, structural, and behavioral. Evidence of long-term impact has been hard to come by. In a recent nationwide examination of cross-sector collaborations for children, for example, Michael Rebell and his colleagues at Columbia University found mixed evidence of their measurable effects when looking at traditional academic success measures ranging from attendance to test scores, grades, graduation rates, disciplinary indictors, and so on.[3] However, measuring student outcomes at scale is different than developing and using more nuanced indicators of children's health and well-being. At the same time, evaluation needs to take into account the effectiveness of Cabinets in promoting not only policy change but more efficient, effective communication and community collaboration for children.

Part of the challenge is that it is difficult to identify what success looks like for complex, cross-sector work. Another factor, though, is the need for more comprehensive guidance on how to create and sustain this kind of collaboration over time. As new communities have joined By All Means, we at EdRedesign have recognized the need for a synthesis of effective practice in cross-section collaboration that brings together practical guidance for initiating and sustaining change with an understanding of the complex realities in which that change occurs. We seek to understand not only what new systems should look like and how they should serve families and children, but how, through collaborative action, we can create such systems in widely varying communities across this country.

This book seeks to contribute what we have learned from our partnership and embedded research with the communities in the By All Means consortium and to introduce a new framework—the Measures of Success framework—and key tools for city, school, and community leaders who want to come together in pursuit of shared goals for students and chart progress against these goals over a sustained period of time.

Throughout the book, we also draw on examples not only from By All Means but from other communities, either in networks or operating independently, all of which illustrate engagement in cross-sector collaborations. These examples illustrate how the collaborative action process can work and be tailored to local circumstances. These communities are diverse geographically and in size, governance structures, political contexts, and demographics. Working with and observing them over time has allowed us to implement a set of experiments and see what enables and hinders progress. Specifically, we draw from two years of interviews with mayors, superintendents, "backbone" or liaison staff (backbone organizations, described in detail later, are typically staffed organizations purposed to carry out day-to-day Cabinet work), and others. We also include illustrations drawn from our regular interactions with and observations of Cabinet meetings.

We would like to acknowledge that in addition to our own research, we have been influenced by the work of the Children's Funding Project, the Forum for Youth Investment, the Collective Impact Forum, and others. We also ground our thinking in the literature on leading change management processes. The eight-step process outlined by John Kotter, a Harvard Business School professor and expert on change management, particularly resonates with the work of leading cross-sector collaboration for children. All the steps of Kotter's process—create a sense of urgency, build a guiding coalition, form a strategic vision and initiatives, enlist a volunteer army, enable action by removing barriers, generate short-term wins, sustain acceleration, and institute change—fundamentally influenced the process and framework described in this book.

The six core chapters of this book lay out strategies and action steps called for by the By All Means collaborative action process to support the long-term success of cross-sector collaborations (see figure I.1). Chapter 1 makes the case that mayors, along with superintendents and other community leaders, should assume leadership in reshaping their communities' commitments to children and youth. Chapter 2 describes the value of creating Children's Cabinets to coordinate and oversee this work and offers guidance on how to structure and implement them. Chapter 3 places equity and community engagement at the center of cross-sector collaboration and suggests strategies for addressing issues of racism and trust. In chapter 4, we

FIGURE I.1 By All Means collaborative action process

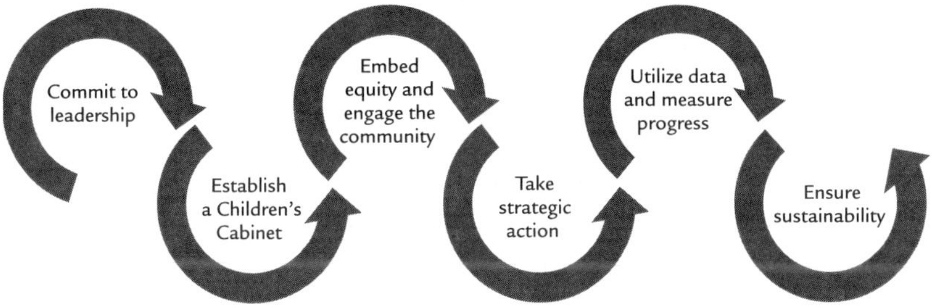

present approaches to taking concrete actions that will make a difference in opportunities and outcomes for children and youth. Chapter 5 highlights the important roles of data and metrics at all stages of the collaborative effort. Chapter 6 illustrates strategies for ensuring long-term sustainability of the effort despite the inevitable obstacles. In chapter 7, we propose strategies for taking advantage of this moment of intersecting crises in the United States to rethink key elements of our current system.

The guidance we offer here is intended to be concrete enough to serve as a road map to help communities adopt cross-sector collaborations in order to implement new systems of support for children and youth, while also recognizing the important role of local context. The embedded examples give insight into how the development of cross-sector collaborations has played out in different communities. Their accomplishments have included important structural changes such as the creation and sustained operation of Children's Cabinets, increased funding for key elements of the cradle-to-career pipeline, and new cross-sector actions that have yielded new opportunities for children and youth. Somerville, Massachusetts, as one example, has raised nearly $3 million to expand high-quality preschools and has more than doubled student participation in afterschool programming. The Cabinet is working to smooth the transition from preschool to the public school system through improved coordination and data and has undertaken a community-wide visioning process called "Somerville Learning 2030." As communities face the vast challenges of addressing children's needs during the pandemic, many are relying on their Cabinets to coordinate the response.

We hope that through such examples, other mayors, superintendents, Cabinet staff, and organizational leaders can each see their respective roles in shaping a cross-sector effort to fit the needs of children and youth in their communities. Finally, we hope that this book inspires these leaders to embrace these new roles in the quest for better ways to serve our children, their families, and our communities.

CHAPTER 1

Commit to Leadership

"Our city can't prosper unless our young people prosper, but simply providing an adequate school experience is not enough to guarantee that the overwhelming majority of our young people will be prepared to be successful. We need to do more." This was the logic that led mayors like Libby Schaaf of Oakland, California; Greg Fischer of Louisville, Kentucky; Jorge Elorza of Providence, Rhode Island; Joe Curtatone of Somerville, Massachusetts; and Kim Driscoll of Salem, Massachusetts to commit to the first cohort of Harvard's By All Means initiative. These mayors, and others subsequently, committed to putting their political and financial capital on the line in order to build a new architecture of support and opportunity systems to complement their improving public education systems and make it possible for all their children to come to school genuinely ready to learn.

Municipal leadership is essential to providing the missing pieces in a holistic strategy to prepare far greater numbers of young people for success in college and careers. Our current, standardized, factory model of education is limited in scope and capacity. Its primary focus is, appropriately, academic achievement, and in recent years school systems have been pressured by federal and state policy makers to achieve world-class standards in core subjects, to close achievement and attainment gaps, and to expand the scope of education to include subjects like twenty-first-century skills and social-emotional learning. The results of more than a quarter century of education reform are in: modest progress in some places, but millions of children graduating who are not ready for either college or a twenty-first-century high-skill, high-knowledge job.

Why has this happened? Not for lack of effort. First, reform mandates were too often unaccompanied by any increase in the capacity (resources, teachers, time) and scope of schooling. For example, K–12 schools still account for only about 20 percent of the typical public school student's waking hours between the ages of five and eighteen, yet policy makers have asked schools to achieve world-class standards while covering an increasing number of subjects in that inadequate allotment of time.

Second, reforms typically focused too narrowly, and sometimes exclusively, on improving curriculum and instruction. That focus sounds like common sense, but it ignores factors that are critically important in determining the success of education. While the core business of education is definitely the transaction between teacher, student, and curriculum, education reform overemphasized improvements to curriculum and teaching while largely ignoring the experiences of students outside of schools. Impediments to student learning such as poverty, trauma, hunger, and inadequate health care, mental health care, and dental care were largely treated as matters beyond the concern of schools. Yet these factors regularly impede the learning process and prevent many students from achieving success in school.

As we argue in the introduction, we believe that local communities are the place to start on this work of developing a new architecture for child development and education, a new design based on a holistic, 360-degree conception of children's developmental needs. We believe in the power of local communities, beyond that of state and federal players, to fashion a new approach to resolving persistent challenges. Particularly in 2020, when our local communities face unprecedented health and economic threats due to the Covid-19 pandemic coupled with enormous pressure to make progress on racial justice, our local jurisdictions are ripe for change and strong leadership. As Benjamin Barber wrote in *If Mayors Ruled the World*, cities are "the most networked and interconnected of our political associations, defined above all by collaboration and pragmatism, by creativity and multiculture."[1]

Mayors are uniquely situated to issue a clarion call to their communities to rally around children and youth, to call on their constituents to address the issues preventing large numbers of youth from realizing their potential and becoming self-supporting adults and informed citizens. While fully dedicated to the necessary and continuous improvement of schooling, mayors have the stature and influence to broaden their community's perspective on the needs of children and how their community can and should do more for its youth than merely providing an adequate school system. Mayors can be the leaders in our nation's adoption of a new paradigm for education: meet each and every child where they are, starting in early childhood, and give them the supports and opportunities they need, inside and outside of school, to succeed throughout their school journey, ultimately attaining some level of postsecondary education that enables them to enter a well-paying job and to embrace informed citizenship.

Clearly, such a paradigm is much easier described than enacted. But "where there is no vision, the people perish."[2] Mayors can bring their communities to the table by attracting all those who care about children's success, from top leaders to grassroots parents. The mayor is well positioned to persuade the entire community that the job of developing and educating children and youth needs the engagement of the entire community. With the guidance of mayors' leadership, communities can formulate a children's agenda, set goals for closing pernicious gaps in opportunities and supports, raise resources, enact strategies, evaluate progress, and hold themselves accountable. Mayors can be the catalyst for a genuine all-community embrace of the work of preparing all children for success. As Mayor Joe Curtatone describes his role:

> I see my role as knowing when to dive in deeper or closer with the people doing the work, and when to step back and allow them to own the work more. When to . . . use my elected position and rhetorical power to spark people to do things, and to be supportive, too, to let them know I'm all-in in helping to lead and support this conversation, knowing that it's okay to take risks, and to be bold.

LEADING A NEW APPROACH

When Greg Fischer took office as Louisville's mayor in 2011, "lifelong learning" was one of three priorities for the city. His background in business had instilled in him a clear understanding of the need for a highly skilled workforce, and his outspoken belief that the city's deep racial inequities needed to be addressed shaped his commitment to ensuring all of Louisville's children had a fair shot at success. Building on an effort already underway to increase the number of college graduates in Louisville, Fischer launched a cradle-to-career initiative. This effort had four pillars, each led by a different local entity: early childhood, K–12 education, higher education, and workforce training. These pillars each developed strategies for contributing to the broad goal of increasing college and postsecondary completion.

Along with these local partnerships, Fischer formed alliances with like-minded national organizations. He joined the newly created By All Means initiative when it formed in 2014, embracing its theory that the effects of poverty on children could not be erased by schools alone and that cross-sector collaboration could lead to better services and supports for children, after learning about it during a National Conference of Mayors convention. He formed and assumed leadership of a Children's Cabinet and participated—along with the superintendent, school board members, heads of the other cradle-to-career pillars, and key civic organizations—in the twice-yearly By All Means meetings. And he built a relationship with the Jefferson County Public Schools superintendent through regular coffee meetings.

Fischer also explored a partnership with Say Yes to Education, whose theory of change pairs "Promise Scholarships" for college with supports and services for children to ensure they are ready to take advantage of those scholarships. While Louisville did not ultimately become a full Say Yes to Education city due to the high cost of funding the scholarships, the city remains committed to its core concepts and continues to work with the Weiss Institute, an affiliate of Say Yes.[3]

Fischer spoke and wrote regularly about the need to improve outcomes for children, including an urgent plea in his state of the city addresses, publishing op-eds, and discussing it during television interviews. He coordinated the development of a memorandum of understanding stating the shared goals of the cradle-to-career effort that was ultimately signed by all organizations represented on the Cabinet. To identify how the different agencies across the city that provide services to children were spending their money, the mayor also supported a fiscal analysis that required data sharing and complex legal agreements. As he said in a 2017 interview, "You need to be concerned about inequity, and you need to see it as a human and economic problem. For me, it's a question of human potential. How much human potential are we leaving on the table when we don't let everyone succeed? If we can agree on that being a problem, then we can get to a new goal."[4]

As the effort progressed, Louisville's cradle-to-career initiative moved from the mayor's office, created a separate 501(c)(3) organization, renamed itself Evolve502, and proceeded to build a sustainable backbone organization—an entity whose role is to provide staffing, fundraising, and operational support to the Cabinet—with an executive director to guide the work.

CREATE A NEW LEADERSHIP PARADIGM

As the Louisville example shows, building cross-sector systems of education and support for children and youth requires bold leadership and new ways of doing business for mayors, superintendents, and the heads of other agencies and organizations. It means mayors taking on new responsibility for children's success and well-being as well as driving the integrative work across sectors in ways that break with traditional operational patterns and procedures. Leadership matters precisely because this work is difficult and requires fundamental changes to organizational cultures and practices. It also necessitates a balance between technical and adaptive leadership moves. Harvard Kennedy School leadership expert Ron Heifetz, who has advised mayors and superintendents throughout the By All Means initiative, has written extensively about the importance of an adaptive mindset that acknowledges the emotional and cultural elements of leading complex change. Mayors and superintendents need to recognize and address the organizational, political, and personal interests of those in the community whose support they seek.

In this chapter, we outline the key leadership moves for both mayors and superintendents. We also offer strategies for creating a broad public movement that can sustain the initiative beyond the tenure of any one leader. Our perspective is that leadership at the highest level of municipal government is required to meet the challenges of preparing our youth for success at scale. Mayors, ideally, should lead this cross-sector initiative. Cities and other local jurisdictions are the logical places to take on this effort. While the school department plays a central and essential role, the vision for this work is broader than the mission and capacities of schools alone. A municipality's top elected or appointed leaders have both the responsibility and the influence to initiate, inspire, and organize this work.

THE ROLE OF MAYORS

As we describe above, mayors and other municipal heads can use their unique positions of authority to create a sense of shared purpose and urgency; to create a coalition for change and collaboration; and to create funding and structural changes that will institutionalize a new, durable system for supporting children, one that can survive leadership turnover.

Make Children's Success and Well-being a Community-wide Responsibility

The initial leadership moves for the mayor are simple on their surface, but they reflect a profound change in practice. The first steps are simply for mayors to choose to make the success and well-being of children a citywide priority and to use their authority and public platform to carry this out. Mayors have both the formal authority and the cachet to determine the high-profile goals for the city, and they have a unique ability to broaden responsibility for children from a few specific agencies to the community as a whole. This should include parents and community members, the health sector, afterschool and summer program providers, social services, and others. This signaling from the mayor, coupled with concrete actions in support of the cross-sector effort, raises its profile, ensures it will be taken seriously, and accelerates the pace of change.

Partner with Superintendents and School Districts

Mayors should form strong alliances with superintendents, school board members, and other key school leaders at the outset of the collaboration. Regardless of whether or not a mayor has authority over the school system, she should assume a leadership role in embracing the community's responsibility for children. While it is important to extend responsibility for children beyond schools and to broaden the range of supports for children beyond the academic, it is also important to acknowledge that schools will continue to play an essential, central role in any cross-sector effort. They remain the primary place children spend their time outside their homes and are often a hub for other services. And while schools alone cannot—and should not be expected to—provide a full set of health, social services, and other supports for children, it is also true that efforts for children cannot succeed without strong schools at the center of the effort. Most school leaders will embrace integrated, community initiatives to address the holistic needs of children, because they recognize that when done well, not only will students directly benefit from these efforts, but these initiatives will free school leaders and teachers to focus their attention on providing a high-quality learning experience rather than addressing the nonacademic challenges children face.

Mayors often have little if any formal authority over schools, and schools and city government frequently operate in separate silos. While there are a few "mayoral control" cities in which mayors have direct responsibility for the schools, mayors more often have a limited role—such as chairing the school board—or none at all. Jurisdictions for municipal governance and school districts may not even align completely: some states, for example, have county-based school districts. In these situations, mayors typically have substantial informal authority and influence. The key for mayors is to use their influence, the bully pulpit, to galvanize public attention, focusing on students' needs while actively supporting schools and students through constructively creating partnerships with superintendents that acknowledge superintendents' authority in the school system. Mayors can also strengthen community collaboration by using their influence to draw a variety of powerful local partners to the collaborative action table.

Create a Public Movement for Children

A major obstacle to systemic changes is a widespread acceptance of the status quo. Mayors should establish a sense of urgency about the need to act, and to act quickly, to address the injustice of unequal opportunity and pervasive, persistent achievement gaps. Children's vastly unequal opportunities and outcomes stay below most people's radar and are relegated to the responsibility of the schools. Public tolerance, and often leadership acceptance as well, of the harsh challenges facing children can feel like the fable about a boiling frog: a frog dropped into boiling water, the story goes, will immediately jump out, but one dropped into water that is heated gradually will stay in until the water boils. Complacency, even if a blind function of inertia, makes leaders and all of us complicit in the continuance of inequity. Too often, we accept as normal, or at least bearable, situations that develop over time. For many reasons, those most impacted by poverty and racial discrimination, those who endure the effects of inequity, are also less likely to have the resources, time, or political capital to advocate for change or to be taken seriously when they do.

This is where leaders come in. After identifying the need for a cross-sector collaboration for children as a priority, mayors should use their multiple platforms to explain why collaborative action is needed and to build a public demand for it. The key to sustaining collaborative initiatives is for this new social compact, this new concept of advancing childhood development, to be embraced by the community and embedded in residents' sense of identity, fairness, and expectations. This is a new social compact wherein communities redefine what they will do collectively for families and children. Mayors should use official messaging opportunities, such as annual state of the city reports, as well as their access to media, public speaking, and other platforms, to make the case for why the city needs to take on broader responsibility for children and what steps the community is taking.

There are several key components to this message.

Create energy and focus on needs

Define a clear and concrete statement of the problem that conveys its urgency. Use a few key data points highlighting trends that are not widely known, such as a rise in attempted suicides by young people, or stark disparities in the current system, such as the gap in kindergarten readiness between different groups of children. Link the data with brief anecdotes that convey the human costs of the current system. Take the opportunity to disaggregate data and point out intolerable gaps based on race, ethnicity, income, or other factors.

Create a mentality of "our kids"

Make clear, as Robert Putnam does in his compelling book *Our Kids*, that the well-being and success of *all* children in the community matters for everyone, whether or not they have children in need, for both economic and moral reasons.[5] Link the need for an educated and competent workforce to building prospering businesses that create jobs and feed the local economy. Talk about the effect of an educated citizenry on everything from creating an appealing community with strong real estate values to the reduction in need for and expenses of social services.

Define a solution in the form of a new way of organizing to meet the challenges

Propose a Children's Cabinet, a broad-based structure that involves multiple agencies, community organizations, local leaders, and others to create a set of mutually reinforcing, coordinated activities to benefit children and youth. Identify the potential goals of a Children's Cabinet and the initiatives that could be undertaken to address them, but make it clear that the Cabinet will have to decide on goals and strategies collaboratively.

Convene a Children's Cabinet

Mayors are uniquely able to bring together key actors, including agency directors, community service providers, unions, parent and other advocacy groups, philanthropies, businesses, and others. Some participants will approach the opportunity of a Cabinet eagerly, while others will be more wary. For example, some service providers will be pleased that their long-standing efforts on behalf of families and children are now being prioritized, but they may also be concerned about what this means for their autonomy and the direction of their work.

To build an effective coalition, mayors need to understand the roles, interests, and history of each of the groups that must take part for this effort to succeed. They or a representative from their office should talk with the heads of each organization and learn what they already do that can contribute and how they envision their role in this new effort. This outreach should involve a sincere desire to learn from those already doing this work. Not everyone will be equally enthusiastic, and some will have legitimate concerns about the implications for their organizations—whether because priorities and funding may be shifting to other areas, or because they expect to be asked to take on additional responsibilities they feel are beyond their capacity, or because they will need to shift their organizational cultures and mindsets. These are legitimate concerns that mayors should take seriously and address. Other organizations may not see an immediate self-interest in the work or may have doubts about collaborative action and the time it consumes. Mayors can be persuasive and should work with each organization to identify a meaningful role in fulfilling the Cabinet's mission.

Raise, Streamline, and Reallocate Funds

The availability of funding is a key factor in starting and sustaining collaborative action, as we discuss in more detail later in the book.

Mayors should use their budgetary authority to prioritize finding, streamlining, and generating new funding that benefits children. This should include both support for a backbone function—a person or organization responsible for organizing the effort, scheduling meetings of the governing body, raising and distributing funds, and ensuring work is being carried out between meetings—as well as for the programmatic initiatives the Cabinet undertakes as part of its work.

The most obvious way for mayors to provide financial support is by allocating funds in their budgets for these purposes. Along with dedicating new money in their budgets, mayors should direct public agencies to coordinate and streamline funding for youth programs to ensure money is being spent as effectively and efficiently as possible. With their public platforms and high profiles, mayors are also particularly well positioned to play a lead role in fundraising efforts.

Commit Staffing

Mayors should support the collaborative action effort by committing staffing support from within their own office as well as signaling that other agencies should do the same. Building staff capacity is essential for the success of collaborative action initiatives. For the Cabinet itself, having backbone support with autonomy from either the mayor or the superintendent is ideal to enable the Cabinet to avoid the perception that it is too closely aligned with just one sector. But each of the major partners in the collaboration also needs to have someone whose job includes dedicating a substantial amount of time to focus on this work.

THE ROLE OF SUPERINTENDENTS

Just as the first step for mayors is to commit to a new way of doing business, superintendents must also decide to approach their work in new ways. While many superintendents commonly struggle with underfunded budgets and welcome the Cabinet's acknowledgment that schools and teachers are being asked to fill needs for which they are neither trained nor funded, some superintendents will find working in collaboration with city governments and other agencies represents a substantial shift and a potential threat. Superintendents also have authority over schools and teachers and must work with their school boards to set the priorities and tone for their districts. For cross-sector collaboration to work, superintendents need to be collaborative in spirit and flexible in the way in which they operate. They must be community-oriented and open-minded about the nature of the challenges facing families and students, while inclined toward partnering with all those who can assist.

Effective partnerships require staffing and staff time, which are often scarce commodities, especially in school systems. Superintendents and those in other agencies and organizations working with them must recognize that being a good partner means meeting halfway, which requires capacity in the form of personnel who are willing, able, and available to engage in active partnership. All parties to Cabinet partnerships should be aware that finding and supporting such staffing is often a challenge for superintendents and other organizations.

Educate the Mayor and Other Community Leaders

Mayors may have a strong desire to better serve children in their communities, but superintendents have made it their careers to do so. Superintendents have deep expertise on children's needs, what their schools do, and what works. They know the many roles teachers are asked to fill and the partnerships that already exist in the schools. They are also extremely well versed in the data on children in their districts: demographic data showing how many of their students are living in poverty, how many require special education or are English language learners, how many are homeless. And as the ones held accountable for students' academic progress and attainment, they know how well children are doing in their districts on reading and math assessments, graduation and dropout rates, and school attendance, overall and for each subgroup of students. Finally, superintendents have deep insight into the challenges facing families and children in the region. Mayors should seek out this expertise and listen to and learn from superintendents and other school leaders about what students and schools need and what the district is already doing.

Superintendents can also work with Cabinet leaders to create a data portrait of the community's children, an important step in creating a clearer understanding of their needs and strengths. Superintendents can make the children's challenges real for mayors and the community at large by telling stories about specific children and the conditions they and their families face. Another key element superintendents can share is the content and nature of the work already being done both inside the school system and out. Often, the mayor and the community are unaware of the range of responsibilities schools have assumed or specific initiatives underway.

Identify the Role the Schools Can Play

Although the point of collaborative action is, of course, to share the responsibility for children's success and well-being broadly across an entire community, schools will continue to play a vital role in these efforts. The goal is for other sectors to partner with schools and complement their work. Accomplishing this represents a culture shift for schools as well as for the community as a whole. School leaders, from the superintendent on, will need to collaborate in new ways and be open to different ideas about how best to meet children's needs holistically. In Illinois, for example, teachers in schools that are part of the Resilient Southern Illinois cross-sector collaboration now hold in-depth individual meetings with students to develop success plans for the transition from middle to high school. Other By All Means communities that have partnered with integrated student support organizations such as City Connects have implemented new processes in schools for assessing students' needs and connecting them with a range of supports. And in Louisville, the Jefferson County Public Schools are rolling out a new data platform that integrates school and social services data to improve referrals to supports and services. Dozens of student support staff will take on this new role.

Identify Areas of Need

Other sectors will need to recognize the vast experience of teachers, principals, and district leaders in child development and education, not to mention their specific knowledge of individual children that can serve as a valuable resource in identifying needs for support and enrichment opportunities. Schools are being asked to fill an increasing number of roles and to provide services beyond their capacity. Teachers see, every day, the challenges their students face that make it difficult for them to focus on learning, from insecure food and housing to experiences of trauma. While more schools are incorporating social-emotional skills into their curricula and cultures, these interventions only help children manage their feelings about the conditions they face without mitigating the challenges themselves. Superintendents need to support teachers and other staff in embracing broader roles while protecting them from being expected to take on an ever-increasing set of responsibilities. Schools desperately need allies in the community who can advocate for the policy and budgetary changes that will improve the lives of children and better prepare them to take advantage of improved schooling.

A first task for superintendents, then, is to identify areas where the children and, by extension, the schools could most benefit from partnership. They may, for example, see unmet mental health needs or kindergarten students lacking the self-regulation needed for more formal schooling as the biggest unmet challenge facing students in their district. Superintendents also need to determine the nature of the partnership the schools are prepared to support and lead the negotiations with various partners on the terms and conditions of new partnerships.

PLAN FOR LEADERSHIP TURNOVER

A risk in relying on mayors and superintendents to drive collaborative action is that the initiative will fail when one or both leaves. Turnover in these top roles is inevitable, and superintendents and mayors should actively plan for their eventual departure by creating a durable legacy through structures embedded in the fabric of the community. We discuss ways to accomplish this in more detail elsewhere, but it is important to see planning for turnover as an explicit leadership goal and responsibility.

Alternatives to Mayoral Leadership

In some communities, mayoral leadership of a Children's Cabinet will not be an effective strategy, and those who want to establish a cross-sector partnership will need to find an alternate structure. As we explain above, mayoral and other top-level leadership can galvanize cross-sector collaboration and raise the profile of the effort in important ways. Because of this, By All Means initially recruited partner cities by identifying mayors who were interested in leading this work in their own communities. We recognize, though, that there are other ways to structure cross-sector collaborations and that these may be preferable in some communities. The Partnership for Resilience in Illinois, for example, began as a collaboration between the Illinois chapter of the American Academy of Pediatrics and Illinois Education Association as a way to address childhood trauma. A second site, Resilient Southern Illinois, now operates in the rural southern region of the state. Both of these sites operate through a steering team without municipal leadership. Other champions in these communities, typically high-profile, trusted community leaders, are often pivotal in starting such collaboratives.

Bringing the Mayor on Board

In situations where the mayor or municipal leader is not the most appropriate leader or convener of a cross-sector collaborative, those who do lead the initiative must endeavor to bring the mayor on board. EdRedesign formed the By All Means initiative by identifying mayors who were *already* committed to making children's well-being a central goal of their tenures. For various reasons, though, this is typically not the case. Since most mayors lack formal authority over the schools, they are often reluctant to wade into the complicated, politically risky territory of improving outcomes for children. Others may simply have identified different priorities.

When the impetus for a collaborative effort for children comes from outside the mayor's office, one of the first tasks is to approach the municipal authorities, including but not limited to the mayor, to enlist their support and cooperation. The leaders of this type of collaboration, one started outside of the mayor's authority, may come from the school system or from other community organizations supporting children such as the United Way, youth coalitions, advocacy groups, and others. Leaders of such a collaborative will need to build the case for collaboration on children's needs to the broader community by combining compelling stories highlighting the breadth of children's issues with data. Finally, they will need to present a bold plan that could become a positive feature for a mayor's tenure or possibly even a signature initiative for a visionary mayor to embrace even if she isn't at the helm. Having a core group committed to taking on the work with a concrete plan for carrying it forward can help the mayor see the value and feasibility of the effort.

As John Donahue and Richard Zeckhauser write in their book on collaborative governance, the "more diligent, honest, and skillful are the leadership and management of the public side, the more successful have been the efforts of collaborative governance."[6] Strong leadership is essential to creating the shared understanding of and cross-sector commitment to solving the systemic challenges of fragmentation, inconsistency and underinvestment that have caused communities' failure to succeed with their most vulnerable children.

Key Tasks for Committing to Leadership

For mayors or other municipal leaders

- Make children's success and well-being a community-wide responsibility
- Partner with superintendents and school districts
- Create a public movement for children
- Convene a community-wide coalition
- Raise, streamline, and reallocate funds
- Commit staffing

For superintendents

- Educate the mayor and other community leaders
- Identify the role the schools can play
- Identify areas of need
- Partner with community leaders and organizations

CHAPTER 2

Establish a Children's Cabinet

Building a new cross-sector system for children and youth requires new ways to align the myriad agencies and organizations with responsibility for young people's education and well-being. In most communities, these sectors are siloed and have limited coordination with, or even understanding of, what the others are doing. School systems generally operate independently of the city government, while the health, social services, recreation, and safety agencies each have their own focus and sphere. Other providers of youth services, such as afterschool and faith-based organizations, offer a patchwork of services that results in both inefficient delivery and unmet needs.

Creating a Children's Cabinet offers a powerful solution to this fragmentation. A Children's Cabinet is an action-focused, executive-level, collaborative body that brings together agencies and organizations to create a coordinated agenda for children and youth. The Cabinet is the lynchpin of the cross-sector collaboration, with responsibility for identifying top priorities and common goals, defining the role each entity can play in achieving them, developing strategies for carrying them out, tracking progress toward the goals, holding parties accountable for making progress, and communicating this progress to the public. Cabinets can also improve the efficiency of the myriad agencies and organizations serving children and youth by enabling them to identify areas of overlap and gaps and to streamline programs and services.

While there are several forms that Children's Cabinets can take, we favor those led by the mayor and codified by a local governing body. Such a Cabinet should include the superintendent and representatives from other entities with responsibility for or interest in children's education, opportunity, and support. We recognize there are risks to this model, which we address elsewhere. Creating a Children's Cabinet has both practical and symbolic value. When agency heads and other executives join the Cabinet, it signals the high priority the community's leaders are putting on the welfare of its children. Structurally and programmatically, Cabinets reshape the way communities serve children by bringing together leaders across sectors to make children's success a community-wide responsibility rather than one that rests primarily with schools.

This idea of bringing comprehensive supports to children is not new. "Community schools," in a number of forms, have existed for decades with the holistic goal of providing students with wraparound services that generally include health care and afterschool enrichment programming, academic support, and in some cases, other social services and multigenerational support as well. What a cross-sector collaboration, led by a Children's Cabinet, brings to this foundation is a systemwide rather than a school-by-school approach. In many districts with community schools, only some schools have these supports, while others do not. Whether or not an individual child will have the opportunity to benefit from them is left to chance or the family's ability to move to the right neighborhood.

The first problem with this one-off approach is that it creates a significant equity issue: it is inherently unfair to provide some children with access to comprehensive services and not others. The second problem is that it is inefficient and puts an unnecessary strain on the capacity of schools, which must each come up with an approach to addressing students' needs, and of providers, who are being contacted by multiple schools to coordinate support. The highly regarded Coalition for Community Schools, for example, prioritizes a systems approach as it works to dramatically expand the number of community schools in the United States, but the challenge of avoiding the pitfalls of school-centric, individual school efforts remains. The role of the Children's Cabinet is to ensure supports and opportunities are available for all children in need rather than just for a few by constructing community-wide systems that will include all children in need irrespective of their school affiliations. The Cabinet is responsible for creating an efficient and effective system of getting quality services to as many children as possible.

Children's Cabinets are also not a new idea, particularly at the state level. The Forum for Youth Investment has coordinated a network of state Children's Cabinets and other cross-sector coordinating bodies for over fifteen years, and several member Cabinets have operated for decades. At the local level, Children's Cabinets and other cross-sector coordinating bodies have proliferated since the publication of John Kania and Mark Kramer's article on collective impact in the *Stanford Social Innovation Review.*[1] EdRedesign, the Forum for Youth Investment, and the Children's Funding Project jointly launched the Local Children's Cabinet Network in 2019 as a forum "for increasing the efficiency and effectiveness of government efforts to improve child and youth outcomes." The three organizations jointly produced a Children's Cabinet Toolkit, from which this chapter draws.[2] Other organizations such as the Tamarack Institute, the Collective Impact Forum, and FSG, a firm that supports collective impact efforts, have also produced materials to support cross-sector coordinating bodies and backbone organizations.

"Collaboration" is easier said than done. It's easy to persuade even relatively diverse constituencies that we have common interests in the success, educational achievement, and well-being of children, but how do we make common cause? If we truly believe we'll go faster and better together than we would alone, just how do we do that? If we want to forge forward on a genuine "children's agenda," then what do we do Monday morning? These are the questions we attempt to address in this chapter by laying out a series of steps for creating and structuring a Children's Cabinet and building infrastructure to support it. These include creating an understanding of urgency; forming partnerships between city and school leadership; choosing what type of Children's Cabinet to create and determining its membership; defining the Cabinet's purpose; focusing meetings on action steps; forming task forces for specific actions; creating a backbone staff role or organization to support the Cabinet; and communicating with the public.

In later chapters, we describe in more detail how Cabinets can carry out and sustain their work.

DECIDE TO FORM A CABINET

The first step in convening a Cabinet is for someone with authority and public standing—often, the mayor—to decide to lead this initiative. In some cases, there is a precipitating event, alarming trend, or specific issue that compels mayoral attention and spurs action. In Denver, for example, Mayor Michael Hancock identifies a period of rising youth violence in the city as a key driver of his creation of Denver's Children's Cabinet. Louisville's Cabinet and cradle-to-career effort grew out of an "urgent need" identified by the Business Leaders for Education to improve the skills of the region's workforce.[3] In Salem, Massachusetts, the school system found itself unexpectedly designated as underperforming by the state after one of its schools failed to meet targets for student progress. This jolted Mayor Kim Driscoll and the Salem Public Schools to rethink how well its children were doing and how to create meaningful structural changes.

With any community-based undertaking, there are important questions about the relative roles of top-down leadership versus grassroots organizing in determining goals and driving actions. While there is no question that broad community involvement and support are essential for the success and longevity of the work, the role of political and civic leadership cannot be underestimated. Elected leaders have the authority and political capital necessary to set priorities and make structural changes in a way community members alone cannot. Government, business, and philanthropic leaders also have access to necessary resources to underwrite action. Starting with top leadership also demonstrates that children's welfare is an undertaking that involves agencies and organizations across the city. At the same time, we recognize the important critiques of leadership-driven models that neglect to understand community priorities or take the time to build broad-based infrastructure. Community participation is essential.

When EdRedesign created the By All Means network, for example, we started by identifying mayors who already recognized that the success of their cities depends on the success of their children, and the success of children requires more than just adequate schools. We looked for leaders who believed that their cities could not prosper unless their young people were successfully prepared to participate fully in the twenty-first-century economy and democracy, and we chose mayors who were willing to dedicate their political and financial capital to this cause. These were leaders who wanted to take the next steps to create new, durable systems to support children's success. In the four years of By All Means, we have found that mayors are willing to continue to be deeply involved in the work of the Cabinets over a sustained period of time, and that this commitment and ongoing participation drives the continued effort of the Cabinet as a whole. While the nature of the involvement has often shifted as the work of the Cabinet has matured, mayoral support—both practically and politically—continues to play an important role.

There are, of course, risks to any initiative linked to a political leader: initiatives closely tied to a specific mayor are at risk of failing when that mayor leaves office. New mayors typically prefer to start their own signature efforts rather than continuing with ones begun by their predecessors. The strategy to counter this is to create durable structures in the form of codified authorization and support for the Cabinet, new funding streams, and established programs—as well as widespread community demand (built through painstaking public engagement efforts) for this cross-sector approach as the new pathway to civic prosperity.

FORM PARTNERSHIPS WITH SCHOOL LEADERSHIP

While a key goal of Children's Cabinets is to share responsibility for children across agencies and organizations, that in no way lessens the central role of schools in the lives of children and youth. We see schools as the hub of a wheel of public supports for children, while the spokes are the other agencies and elements of the community working with them. Schools are where kids spend most of their time outside their homes, and they are *the* commonly accepted agency for serving children. Ultimately, it is the schools that are held accountable by the state and federal governments and by community members for children's success. For these reasons, schools are the natural curators of supports and services for children, but as currently constituted, they lack the capacity to do all this work themselves.

Establishing strong working partnerships with the school superintendent and key school board members is, therefore, essential to the success of the Children's Cabinet. Top school leadership needs to be a central part of identifying needs and solutions, avoiding redundancy of effort, and defining what types of additional supports are most needed. Much of the work of the Children's Cabinet is to expand on school department work and coordinate services more effectively with the school system. To this end, the mayor should make it a top priority to signal clearly that the goal is to support and enhance the schools' ability to serve students, not to supplant it.

One caveat for working with superintendents, though, is the unpredictable length of their tenures. Of the original six superintendents in the By All Means consortium, for example, only two remain, despite the fact that stability was one of the criteria we considered when forming the initial cohort. In contrast, five of the six original mayors remain in office. This uncertainty is another reason for mayors or other top municipal leaders to take the more central leadership role in the Cabinet. Turnover in the superintendent's role has not derailed the overall work of the Children's Cabinet in any of the By All Means communities, although in some cases it has led to a shift in priorities.

CHOOSE WHAT TYPE OF CABINET TO CREATE

Organizationally, Cabinet membership can reflect a narrow or broad set of stakeholders. They typically take one of three general forms, which are not rigid in their distinctions: a governmental Cabinet, a collaborative Cabinet, or a public Cabinet. In a governmental Cabinet, only municipal agencies have an official seat at the table. Collaborative Cabinets add representatives from major coalitions and network leaders who represent larger groups of people or organizations serving children. Public Cabinets are the broadest, with representatives from business, philanthropies, community agencies representing those the Cabinet intends to serve, members of the community such as parents or students, and others who have an interest but not necessarily a formal role in providing opportunities for youth. There are obviously advantages and disadvantages to each. The governmental model lends itself to more streamlined decision-making and action but generally lacks community involvement, while the collaborative model lends itself to broader participation and buy-in reflecting a more inclusive, but potentially more cumbersome, structure. Given the importance of community voice in this effort, communities that choose a governmental model should build in structures for meaningful community engagement. Determining the best Cabinet structure is also a function of the organizational role the Cabinet will serve—whether to streamline government, advise the mayor and council, make executive decisions, and so on.

Denver's Children's Cabinet, for example, is primarily governmental, with the goal of bringing together all the agencies in the city to share in the responsibility for children's success and to ensure municipal budgets that impact children in any way are aligned around the Cabinet's goals. Mayor Hancock created it in 2012 via executive order, shown in figure 2.1. There is representation on the Cabinet from the schools as well, although the superintendent is not an official Cabinet member. A separate body, the Mayor's Education Compact,

FIGURE 2.1 Denver Children's Cabinet executive order

TO: All agencies under the Mayor
FROM: Michael B. Hancock, Mayor
DATE: July 17, 2012
SUBJECT: Denver Children's Cabinet

Purpose: This Executive Order establishes the Denver Children's Cabinet as the policy making group to coordinate city-based programs and services in order to create opportunities for Denver's children and youth to succeed.

1. **Applicable Authority:** The applicable authority relevant to the provisions and requirements of this Executive Order No. 139 is found in Sections 2.2.1, 2.2.6 and 2.2.10 of the charter and Sections 2-141 to Sections 2-145 of the Revised Municipal Code of the City and County of Denver.
2. **Mission:** The Denver Children's Cabinet will improve communication between agencies, coordinate and align programs and services, and develop strategies to address gaps and remove barriers that hinder opportunities for Denver children and youth.
3. **Members:** The Denver Children's Cabinet shall be comprised of department and agency heads whose departments directly impact Denver children and youth through funding, policies, programs, and or services, including quasi-city or related agencies that affect the lives of Denver children and youth. The Mayor will designate specific departments and agencies whose leaders will be members of the Children's Cabinet by a memorandum attachment to the Executive Order.
4. **Chair:** The Director of Children's Affairs shall be the chair of the Children's Cabinet.
5. **Responsibilities:** The Denver Children's Cabinet shall develop and provide policy guidance and coordinate the integration of services for children and youth across City agencies and their partners. The Children's Cabinet shall:
   - 5.1. Create and maintain an updated inventory of programs and services offered for children and youth, and quantify the City's investment in these programs.
   - 5.2. Identify areas where coordination will lead to better services and more opportunities and implement improvements.

5.3. Identify improvement opportunities within City services and implement plans to address them.

5.4. Establish a broad set of children's metrics that establish the baseline for child well-being in Denver from which to measure progress towards desired outcomes.

5.5. Integrate Department and Agency Peak Performance strategic plans, and the performance metrics contained in these plans, to support and achieve the children's metrics to the extent appropriate.

6. **Memorandum Attachments:** The procedures for implementing this Executive Order may be defined by Memorandum Attachments to the Executive Order which shall become part of the Executive Order. Further, the Children's Cabinet shall have the authority to issue procedural Memorandum Attachments relative to the Executive Order.

has broad representation from community organizations, higher education, and others, but acts as an advisory board for specific topics. Louisville's Cabinet reflects the other end of the spectrum, with its membership including the superintendent of schools, higher education, community-based organizations, workforce development, and local philanthropies.

Oakland had two cross-sector bodies focused on children when it joined By All Means: the Youth Ventures Joint Powers Authority (YVJPA), a county-based group with state-based legal authority to coordinate services across government entities, and the Oakland Thrives Leadership Council, an advisory group to the YVJPA with a broader membership, including community and faith-based organizations, philanthropies, health-care organizations, and others. Ultimately, this dual structure has proven unwieldy, and the city has been in the process of merging and restructuring to create a single body that reflects a public Cabinet model.

The Children's Cabinet Toolkit describes the Cabinet types in more detail, as shown in figure 2.2.[4]

FIGURE 2.2 Options for Children's Cabinets

WHO WILL THE MEMBERS OF THE CABINET BE?

OPTION 1
Governmental cabinet
CABINET MADE UP OF
- Municipal departments and agencies such as the parks and recreation department

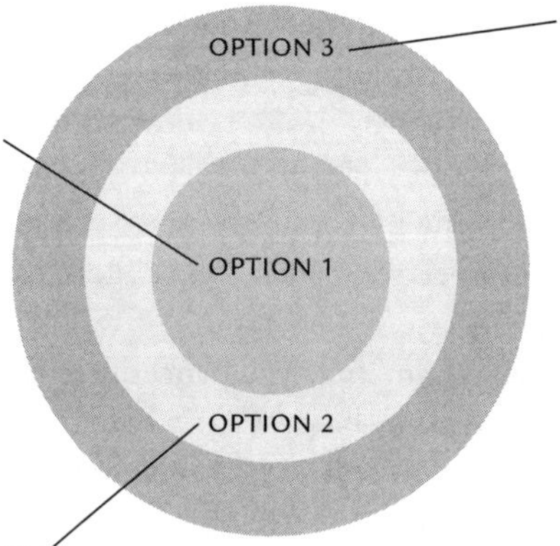

OPTION 3
Public cabinet
CABINET MADE UP OF
- Business leaders
- Unions
- Civic leaders
- For-profit institutions
- Advocates
- Parents
- Youth
- Philanthropy

OPTION 2
Collaborative cabinet
CABINET MADE UP OF
- Coalitions, collaboratives, intermediaries, or collective impact groups focused on children, youth, and families
- Representatives of major public stakeholder groups (health/medical, early childhood, higher education, local business association, Chamber of Commerce, providers, etc.)

CHOOSE IF:
OPTION 1
Your primary or initial goal is to break down cross-agency silos and better coordinate people, data, and money within your municipal government.

This option will yield the smallest Children's Cabinet. Benefits of a small cabinet include consistency of participation and accountability, more flexible and nimble speed of progress, and all voices being heard.

Note: In this structure, other stakeholders (providers, intermediaries, business leaders, advocates, parents, etc.) provide input through participation in subcommittees or community forums.

OPTION 2
Your goal is to foster collaboration across municipal agencies and with non-governmental stakeholder groups.

OPTION 3
You want to take advantage of opportunities to collaborate with civic and business leaders who can leverage the power of people or resources to make change.

You want to provide a forum for community discussion and incorporate a diverse range of voices into your discussions.

Challenges are associated with larger cabinets. Cabinets that include the maximum number of voices are better able to identify a diverse range of perspectives, but also may risk losing participation, speed of progress, accountability, and focus.

Examples

Option 1 Denver Children's Cabinet

As mandated by executive order:

- Director of Children's Affairs;
- Managers of Dept. of Human Services, Parks and Recreation, Safety, Finance, Environmental Health, Community Planning and Development;
- Chief of Police;
- Directors of Corrections and Undersheriff, the Office of Economic Development, PeakPerformance, the Office of Strategic Partnerships, Development Services, Denver's Road Home, Career Service Authority, Denver Housing Authority, Community Health Services;
- City Council Member;
- City Librarian;
- Denver Public Schools representative;
- Denver Preschool Program representative;
- and a board member of the Scientific and Cultural Facilities District.

Option 2 Fairfax Successful Children and Youth Policy Team

- Fairfax County Public Schools board and administration members (9),
- Fairfax County Government county board and administration (10),
- Community Members (15) (including voices from early childhood, faith-based organizations, families, health care, business, philanthropy, nonprofits, higher education, advocacy, and out-of-school time.

Option 3 Louisville Evolve502

Initial cabinet members included at least one high-ranking representative from the pillar lead organizations—Metro United Way, JCPS, 55,000 Degrees, and KentuckianaWorks—in addition to Mayor Greg Fischer, Superintendent Hargens, and representatives from the school board, city government, health care, higher education, and many local nonprofits, businesses, and foundations.

DETERMINE CABINET MEMBERSHIP

Once a community has decided which type of Cabinet it will create, there are two key issues to consider when determining who should serve on it: first, which agencies, organizations, and other constituencies will be represented, and second, whether the Cabinet will comprise top executives or staff members. When the Cabinet includes the mayor or top municipal leader and the heads of key agencies and organizations, it sends a clear message to everyone within those organizations that this is an important effort. Having top leadership on the Cabinet also ensures that the Cabinet includes those with direct decision-making and budgetary authority. On the other hand, top executives are not usually the ones who will actually carry out the day-to-day work.

When Louisville first formed its Children's Cabinet, everyone was welcome to participate. With the mayor signaling this as a major initiative and a solid history in the city of focusing on education and workforce issues, participation at Cabinet meetings ballooned to as many as forty people representing city and county government, the public schools, higher education, philanthropies, community-based organizations, public safety, social services, and others. While this approach enabled broad participation, it also made Cabinet meetings unwieldy, and it was difficult to find a table big enough to seat everyone.

After a few meetings, the Cabinet's facilitator at the time, an organizational change consultant, worked with a core group to set up new ground rules: only the top executives of organizations would be official members of the Cabinet with a direct seat at the table. Other staff could attend the meetings but would not be voting members and would only sit at the table if their boss couldn't attend. A small team that included a mix of Cabinet members and staff met weekly to carry the work forward between Cabinet meetings. While Louisville's Cabinet structure has evolved further since then, this solution shrank the Cabinet by more than half and enabled the group to be more productive.

As the Louisville example shows, Cabinet membership can pose challenges in balancing the need for representation of youth-serving organizations and key community leaders with the need to ensure broad representation of the community, through organizations representing grassroots constituencies as well as people from groups that will be impacted by the Cabinet's policies and programs. The number of Cabinet members can quickly balloon to a size that makes deliberation and nimble decision-making difficult; however, limiting membership too much can decrease community involvement and representation. Collective impact work has sometimes been appropriately criticized for being too "grass tops" at the expense of grass roots, and not truly reflective of the needs or lived experiences of the people being served. It is imperative that Cabinet leaders make their Cabinets reflective of the makeup of their communities and adjust membership over time as needed.[5] They also should initiate other strategies for community inclusion, such as a community council and listening meetings in the community. We discuss these in detail in chapter 3.

Over time, there will inevitably be turnover in Cabinet membership, either because someone new has taken over an existing role or because the Cabinet has added new organizations. One way to ease the onboarding process for new members is to create a "journey map" that documents key decisions and actions over the course of the collaboration. There are many versions of journey maps with different levels of detail and specificity, but we have found that using them can help both new and long-term Cabinet members see the history of the effort and understand the thinking behind different elements of the work. It is also important to recognize that Cabinets, like all organizations, develop a culture. When there is turnover, expect and be open to some changes to that culture so new members become equal partners, while respecting the efforts and decision processes that have already taken place.

DEFINE THE CABINET'S PURPOSE

The first task for the Cabinet is to clarify its purpose and broad common objectives as well as potential points of entry into the work. Defining the purpose both in terms of the community's pressing needs, grounded in data, and in the more personal experiences of Cabinet members and individual community members creates a compelling foundation for the effort. We have found that taking the time for individual Cabinet members to describe on a personal level what brings them to this work grounds the Cabinet's work in the participants' lived experiences and deep knowledge of the community. Whether Cabinet members have themselves grown up in poverty or have a different point of entry for this work, these stories help create a culture within the Cabinet of mutual understanding that everyone shares the same broad mission, even if they sometimes differ on how to achieve it.

Getting concrete about the Cabinet's shared purpose often requires some negotiation and finesse. In some cases, as we note earlier in the chapter, there is a specific event that precipitates the creation of a collaborative effort and leads naturally to a defined purpose. Louisville, for example, had already identified a citywide goal of increasing the college attainment rate before forming its Cabinet, making the primary focus of that work easy to identify. Choosing a specific goal has the advantage of creating a clear focus for the work that people in both the community and the Cabinet can understand and toward which they can direct their energy. Broad, less-specific statements of purpose, such as "all children are healthy and academically successful," are less useful operationally because the end result is not clearly defined. It is important to balance the focus on shared, tangible goals with the understanding that the process of getting there involves the mundane work of developing more streamlined communications, data, and funding structures across departments to support a broad vision of what it takes to support child and youth success.

The overarching goal for most Cabinets is often some version of getting kids to and through college or postsecondary training, since success for children ultimately means they become self-supporting adults who can be productive, healthy, and active members of their communities. What is important, though, is for the Cabinet and public to understand these long-term goals are not just academic and school-based in nature. Improving graduation and postsecondary attainment rates takes a broad, cross-sector set of strategies and actions involving many agencies and organizations in addition to schools, from health to social services to out-of-school enrichment opportunities to philanthropy. This was a lesson learned early in the Promise Scholarship movement: simply removing financial barriers to college was not enough to ensure students would be prepared to go, or to succeed once they got there. They needed a system of supports and opportunities, ideally from birth through postsecondary attainment. We will discuss how communities can develop strategies for achieving their goals in the next chapter.

DEVELOP A BALANCED STRATEGY

In defining a mission and selecting strategies for achieving it, Cabinets need to be mindful of striking a balance between the important work of improving communication and increasing effective collaboration on the one hand and, on the other, devoting time to the advocacy and policy work necessary to change the policies and investments that have led to profound inequalities in our society. Treating both the symptoms and the causes of inequity is fundamental to the goal of providing a cradle-to-career pipeline of education, support, and opportunity that allows every child the chance to succeed. Tackling programmatic, service-oriented work simultaneously with policy advocacy work requires significant capacity, and Cabinet builders will have to assess their capacity and set priorities accordingly.

CREATE A BACKBONE FUNCTION

In collaborative action, the backbone is the structure that, as the name suggests, provides essential support to the work of the Children's Cabinet in the form of staff people or a separate organization, often a 501(c)(3). The backbone structure can be as simple as a single person or as complex as a highly staffed organization. Whatever its form, the backbone role is crucial both for the day-to-day functioning of the Cabinet and for ensuring long-term sustainability. Its role is to ensure the Cabinet has dedicated staffing for implementation and the necessary organizational support to succeed. Cabinet members are inevitably busy with their primary jobs and many responsibilities outside of the operation of the Cabinet. The backbone staff, on the other hand, are those who wake up each day focused on leading the execution of the collaborative work of the Cabinet and prompting Cabinet members to fulfill their respective commitments. But this crucial role is not simply to operationalize a vision: the backbone must also keep a clear focus on the reason the Cabinet exists in the first place, reminding the Cabinet of its mission and connecting its aspirations to its daily work.

During the early stages of a collaboration, backbone support may take the form of an individual acting as a Cabinet coordinator who schedules and may facilitate Cabinet meetings, takes minutes, and follows up to ensure action steps are carried out. It may also take the form of shared responsibilities and tasks between several organizations. As the initiative develops, though, the Cabinet should create a more robust and sustainable backbone structure. One way to do this is for several agencies to pool resources to support a staff position, which can also help get initial organizational buy-in. Another is to form a nonprofit organization with the ability to raise money and carry out a variety of tasks in support of the initiative. Louisville, for example, has created a 501(c)(3) organization as its backbone to support its Evolve502 (502 is Louisville's area code) cross-sector effort and has raised funds that currently support an executive director and other staff. At their most robust, backbone organizations organize, execute, and communicate publicly the work of the Cabinet.

The backbone has a substantial relational component as well. Both research and our own experiences have borne out the importance of strong relationships built on trust to carry out systems change and sustain it over time. It is the role of the backbone to serve as the connective tissue between leaders of organizations with different functions, priorities, and cultures and to develop strong working relationships across multiple sectors and between the community and public agencies.

Because of this mix of responsibilities, choosing the right backbone staff is crucial to the success of the collaboration. The lead staff person—often the executive director or Cabinet coordinator—needs to have the trust, confidence, and respect of the mayor, superintendent, and other key Cabinet and community members. They should be comfortable coordinating and even running meetings of high-level executives. They must also have a strong focus on achieving tangible progress, engaging authentically with a broad community, and creating meaningful relationships. It is important for the backbone leader to be perceived as a neutral, honest, and trustworthy broker who represents the interests of the entire Cabinet rather than one particular element of it. Even when Cabinet members come to the table with the best of intentions, it can be hard to entirely avoid concerns about which sectors will see programmatic or budgetary increases or decreases as a result of the Cabinet's work; if the backbone staff are closely tied to one sector, it increases the likelihood that priorities will be regarded as politically driven or functions of self-interest.

FOCUS MEETINGS ON ACTION STEPS

Cabinet meetings should be action-focused, productive, "can't miss" events. Figure 2.3 offers an example of a Cabinet agenda. Often, the person who runs the meetings and sets the agendas is the backbone staff person or organizational lead, in consultation with the mayor and other key members. In the early stages of the Cabinet, these meetings include defining its broad goals, crafting vision and mission statements, examining data and assets to determine areas of greatest need and opportunity, selecting strategies and points of entry, and identifying long-term measures of success the Cabinet will track over time. For some Cabinets, this data analysis has included mapping financial expenditures against priorities; in others, it has focused more on student outcomes and opportunities.

As the Cabinet takes on concrete actions, meetings should focus on tracking movement toward the goals and making decisions about

FIGURE 2.3 Sample Cabinet meeting agenda

Agenda

- 9:00–9:05 Welcome + Roll Call
- 9:05–9:15 Reviewing Poughkeepsie's Data
- 9:20–9:40 Group Brainstorm
- 9:45–9:55 Review of Metrics of Success
- 9:55–10:25 Identifying Potential Metrics
- 10:25–10:30 Close

Community Agreements

- Building community together is more important now than ever
- Multiple ways of knowing
- Speak plainly and if you don't know, ask!
- Engage with radical imagination & new possibilities
- E.L.M.O—everyone let's move on
- Speak from your own experience
- One mic! Take space/Make space
- What's said here, stays here; what's learned here, leaves here
- Self care and community care—pay attention to yourself, pay attention to your neighbors
- Yes/and, both/and

Source: Poughkeepsie Children's Cabinet

next steps. Cabinets should regularly use the Measures of Success framework (see chapter 5) or another accountability mechanism to assess their progress on both the systemic elements of the work—such as committed leadership, collaboration, and sustainable staffing and funding—and the programmatic ones. It is important for all Cabinet members to have a role in furthering the effort and to see the value of their ongoing participation.

USE TASK FORCES TO ADVANCE SPECIFIC ACTION AREAS

One way to address the need for active, sustained community engagement while carrying forward specific elements of the Cabinet's priorities is to create task forces or working groups. Even for Cabinets that meet frequently, there just is not enough time during meetings to do the kind of deep planning and implementation work necessary to make real, systemic changes. Task forces also enable broader community representation and ensure that people with expertise in particular areas help shape specific initiatives.

These subgroups can change over time as the work matures to ensure the right people are involved at different stages of the effort. In Somerville, for example, subgroups have focused on health, out-of-school time, and early childhood education, while Louisville has formed subgroups to lead the creation of a data platform and to raise the money for its backbone organization, Evolve502. In Denver, Mayor Hancock formalized a five-subgroup structure focusing on data, innovation, policy, budget, and a child safety net in a 2019 addendum to the original executive order establishing the Children's Cabinet.

COMMUNICATE THE EFFORT TO THE COMMUNITY

Building a cross-sector effort requires buy-in from a wide range of audiences. Having a clear message, tailored to the concerns of different audiences, can help convince people to join or support the Cabinet and its efforts. At the heart of this communications strategy is articulating a value proposition—that is, understanding the challenges the community is facing and articulating them clearly, coupled with outlining a credible plan for addressing them. To build an understanding of, and sense of urgency for, the challenges facing children and youth, Cabinets should use a combination of data, statements of values, and links between the success of children and communities as a whole. The Graduate Tacoma effort, for example, uses a creative mix of publicly visible messages—it put small flags all over the community with its logo and contact information for learning more, directly encouraged individual schools and program sites through activities like sending cakes to schools to celebrate successes, and published a compelling annual report that everyone involved in the effort can use to share a common message about goals and progress.

BE FLEXIBLE

While we have noted the need for flexibility, it warrants highlighting. The kind of long-term, sustained change Cabinets are undertaking will inevitably lead to modifications in everything from Cabinet and backbone structure over time to shifts in leadership and community priorities. Successful implementation of some elements of the Cabinet's priorities will mean they eventually require less Cabinet-level attention, while other new priorities will take center stage. As strategies and programs change, people's involvement will as well. This includes the mayor's role; as the work becomes more fully established, the mayor may shift from driving the effort to having more of a support function.

RECOGNIZE ALTERNATE GOVERNANCE STRUCTURES

While we have made a case in chapter 1 for collaborative action to be led by mayors and driven by cross-sector Cabinets that include broad community participation, we know there are instances where this is not feasible or desirable, or where prior decisions have led to the development of a different form of Cabinet. In northern Illinois, for example, the Partnership for Resilience (the Partnership) began as a collaboration between the executive director of the Illinois Education Association and the chief medical officer of a children's hospital. Rather than a Cabinet with governmental representation, the Partnership is governed by a steering committee whose membership includes a number of school districts south of Chicago, the Illinois chapter of the National Academy of Pediatrics, and higher-education institutions. In Tacoma, Washington, the Graduate Tacoma Collective Impact initiative is overseen by the board of directors of the Foundation for Tacoma Students, which is its backbone organization. Mayor Victoria Woodards and Superintendent Carla Santorno both sit on the board, but neither is the leader of the effort. The mayor sees her role as that of an enthusiastic supporter who has been involved since before she assumed her current role. At the same time, the superintendent drives the implementation of substantial parts of the work such as the STEAM Learning Network, which aims to increase interest and opportunity in science and technology for students of color, girls, and those living in poverty. The superintendent also leads the College Support Network, which engages students and families beginning in middle school to develop a college-going identity and provide supports for applying to postsecondary opportunities, such as resources on understanding and applying for financial aid programs.

CONCLUSION

This chapter has outlined some ways and means of organizing and structuring the complex, cross-sector work of integrating supports and opportunities for children. We have described strategies and structures to guide cocreated, local work to benefit children. These structures, such as Children's Cabinets, create new relationships between concerned partners in our communities. The approach to this work will look different in different communities and be adapted to the assets, needs, history, politics, and leadership of those communities.

Sometimes, this work is "leadership without authority," concerned leaders and citizens coming together to address urgent community needs without a particular government mandate.[6] At other times, communities step up and formally authorize and prioritize this work. In any event, we contend that the future success of our society, economy, democracy, and culture depends on our capacity to nurture and develop the talent in all our young people. Local, state, and national leaders need to embrace this challenge in whatever way seems the best fit for their respective constituencies and communities.

Finally, the work is about strategy and action, not just about better communication or working more closely together. Children have pressing needs that must be met, but those needs are often caused by larger problems created by faulty policies and inadequate resources, problems like inadequate health care, food deserts, and pervasive mental illness that need the full attention of our communities, states, and the federal government. If we only come together to make incremental progress, then we will have wasted the opportunity. Now is the time for urgency, action, and dramatic steps forward to ensure that each and every child has what they need to be successful inside and outside of school. These steps should include building out vital services and supports as well as altering insidious policies that guarantee widespread inequity.

Key Tasks for Creating a Children's Cabinet

- Create a sense of urgency
- Form partnerships between cities and school leadership
- Choose what type of Cabinet to create
- Determine Cabinet membership
- Define the Cabinet's purpose
- Focus meetings on action steps
- Use task forces to carry out specific action areas
- Create a backbone function
- Communicate the effort to the public

CHAPTER 3

Embed Equity and Engage the Community

The impetus to form a cross-sector collaboration for children almost always originates from a deep concern about equity. Mayors, superintendents, and other community leaders recognize that many children are on paths that will limit their lifetime opportunities and that schools cannot change this reality on their own. They know the strong correlation between race, poverty, neighborhoods, and the likelihood of success. These leaders take on the difficult and time-consuming work of changing their priorities and practices because they believe that, if they get it right, they will improve the life trajectories for the children in their communities and, in so doing, make their cities, towns, and counties better places to live for everyone. In short, they want to give everyone a real chance at the American dream.

These good intentions are not, in themselves, enough to achieve change. To create systems of opportunity for *all* children, racial and economic equity needs to be at the heart of and embedded into all collaborative efforts by the Children's Cabinet. And despite the strong overlap between poverty and race, addressing race explicitly matters for achieving equity. We write this chapter against the backdrop of intense civil unrest in the aftermath of several deaths of Black people at the hands of White police or vigilantes. This moment—which is the culmination of countless ones before it—makes clear that racism continues to define the United States and impede progress on every front. This is true of the country as a whole, and it is true of each jurisdiction within it. This country's history of racism pervades nearly every aspect of daily life for people of color and is deeply intertwined with the inequitable opportunities and outcomes among children.

As Michael McAfee, Angela Glover Blackwell, and Judith Bell of PolicyLink write in *Equity: the Soul of Collective Impact*, "Equity, both racial and economic, must be infused through all aspects of collective impact processes, from the deep engagement of communities to the collection and analysis of data; the design and scale of solutions; and the capacities, point of view, and roles of backbone organizations."[1] What authentic community engagement and equity work look like will differ across communities. In this chapter, we share strategies that communities have used effectively to address equity challenges. These include acknowledging and engaging with their own communities' histories and experiences of racial inequity; naming equity as an explicit goal; using data and metrics to understand existing disparities and to see the impact of interventions for specific groups of children and youth; ensuring community representation on the Cabinet; engaging families; using multiple strategies to engage the community; and taking a design-thinking approach to incorporating equity into all aspects of the Cabinet's work.

ACKNOWLEDGE YOUR COMMUNITY'S HISTORY AND CURRENT REALITY

An important foundational step for addressing equity is knowing and acknowledging the racial history and economic divides of your city or town. What has been its experience of legal and informal segregation, busing, redlining, and policing? What is the more recent history of economic investment and government commitment to addressing neighborhood and community concerns? In most communities across the United States, race and economic status continue to define opportunity and outcomes. The neighborhood in which a family lives usually correlates directly with their socioeconomic status. Neighborhoods that have been historically marginalized by racial discrimination and inequitable policies affecting housing, health, food, the environment, transportation, jobs, and other factors will most likely be home to the community's most impoverished citizens. As Tony Iton, senior vice president of the California Endowment, has shown through his research, a person's zip code is a strong predictor of their life outcomes in health, education, and other areas.[2] Raj Chetty and his colleagues have similarly shown the reliability of neighborhood as a predictor of a child's life outcomes.[3]

Communities of color have many reasons for skepticism about the sincerity or effectiveness of government intervention. If community leaders and the Cabinet as a whole explicitly acknowledge this, it signals their understanding that they will need to build trust through action and accountability. This is a good place to begin.

NAME EQUITY AS YOUR GOAL

Naming equity as an explicit goal of your cross-sector collaboration elevates its importance and centers the work on equity. In doing this, Cabinets will need to decide how they will collectively define and talk about equity. Is "equity" shorthand for addressing racism? For a broader concern with multiple forms of inequity? Using a more generic framing can be more inclusive, since disparities exist along multiple dimensions, but keeping a broader lens can also dilute the focus and impact. In either approach, it is important to be specific about the disparities between different groups and about concrete equity goals.

The Multnomah County, Oregon All Hands Raised collaboration has grounded its work in racial equity since its inception. Its website states, "Racial equity remains our highest priority. Young people of color make up half of all youth in Multnomah County, but their outcomes consistently lag behind their White counterparts. If we continue to fail kids of color, the social and economic consequences for our community are dire. We must continue to combine the efforts of organizations and individuals who work tirelessly but too often have worked alone."[4]

Chattanooga 2.0, the backbone organization for the Chattanooga–Hamilton County Children's Cabinet, has committed to putting equity at the center of its work and has developed a definition of what this means: "Chattanooga 2.0 defines educational equity as intentional supports, resources, and policies designed to meet the individual needs of each learner and eliminate disparities in outcomes, ultimately ensuring that all students have the opportunity to unlock their full potential."[5] Some other cross-sector collaborations, such as Graduate Tacoma, have adopted a set of commitments or policies addressing equity. Their backbone organization, the Foundation for Tacoma Students, has defined how it intends to operationalize equity in its work, as shown in figure 3.1.

USE DATA AS A TOOL TO UNDERSTAND AND IMPROVE EQUITY

Cabinets should recognize and use the impact of data for identifying equity issues, elevating public awareness, targeting solutions, and shining an equity spotlight on the impact of interventions. One of the most powerful equity tools at communities' disposal is the ability to disaggregate data by racial, ethnic, economic, and other subgroups.

Identify the Nature and Scope of Existing Disparities Through a Gap Analysis

By examining and reporting disaggregated data, communities can demonstrate the scope of inequity and disparate opportunity across communities. Hidden beneath top-line, average trends of all kinds—graduation rates, health outcomes, crime rates, birth weight, kindergarten readiness, academic assessments—are very different stories

FIGURE 3.1 Foundation for Tacoma Students equity commitments

Operationalizing Equity

Equity is an approach. Equity recognizes that we do not all start from the same place because advantages and barriers exist. Equity is a process. By acknowledging these varied starting places, FFTS seeks to correct the imbalance for the most marginalized and minoritized populations.

Equity Commitments

1. Focusing on populations furthest from meaningful opportunities.
2. Disrupting and dismantling structural and institutional racism and systems that result in oppression.
3. Aligning and directing resources to populations under-resourced.
4. Representing the community in which FFTS serves, and at all levels.
5. Redress past systemic and institutional practices by partnering and contracting with women-owned businesses and businesses owned and operated by people of color.

for different groups of children. To enable clearer understanding of the current reality means leaders must incorporate metrics on conditions, opportunity, and access so that Cabinets and communities can clearly perceive the many factors that lead to disparate outcomes. We know, for example, that education achievement and attainment have everything to do with opportunity. Consequently, in collecting data on educational performance, we must not just look at outcomes but at the availability of opportunities. In their absence, it is unreasonable to expect strong academic achievement outcomes.

Leaders should devise data analytics on access to opportunity that include everything from neighborhood safety to the accessibility of preschool, health care, summer and afterschool learning, adequately funded schools, rigorous curricula, and so on. Cabinets need to harness this concrete information to create a picture of life for children in their communities by asking a series of questions and using the answers to make the case for change. Some of the questions that Cabinets should ask are: Where are the biggest disparities in outcomes between children in different racial and economic groups? Where are the biggest disparities in opportunity? How is a child's neighborhood related to opportunity and outcomes? What are the trends over time?

Follow the Money

Inequitable funding is one of the key ways the current system institutionalizes discrimination against students of color and those living in poverty. Examining where money is being spent and how tells a story of that community's commitment to equity, pro and con, and should be a foundational part of the gap analysis. This scan should extend to the resources available in each school, the opportunities for afterschool and summer programming, spending on recreational facilities and parks, the availability of health-care facilities, and as many other services impacting children and youth as possible.

Pinpoint Where Intervention Is Most Needed

Cabinets can use this gap analysis to target interventions to where they are most needed and where they will have the most impact on reducing inequity. In Louisville, for example, a group tasked by the Cabinet with addressing an increase in high school expulsions discovered a huge difference in expulsion rates for Black and White students, and also a disparity in the type of alternative settings Black and White students attended. Data from the US Department of Education's Civil Rights Data Collection revealed that in the Jefferson County Public Schools, Black students represented 67 percent of expulsions despite making up just 37 percent of the student body. This information was part of the impetus by the Louisville Cabinet for the creation of a working group on addressing racial disparities in suspensions and expulsions and the broader issues of behavioral health.

Additionally, as we discuss elsewhere in this book, Denver's leaders have made innovative use of neighborhood-based data visualizations, creating compelling and nuanced portraits of disparity. The Cabinet uses this material as a foundation on which to make decisions about funding and program priorities.

Use an Equity Lens When Reporting on Metrics and Evaluating Impact

Cabinets should use an equity lens when reporting on metrics and evaluating the impact of interventions. Analyses and reporting of Cabinet and program impact should report data on access to services, program participation, and child-level outcomes by race and economic status as well as disability and English learner status. This means, again, disaggregating data to provide a clear picture of who is benefiting and to what extent. To be able to do this, programs need to ensure they collect demographic indicators when gathering data about participation and outcomes. This entails using existing student identifiers to collect participation and outcome data, since doing so enables program data to be linked to the vast amount of student data collected by school districts. For example, a summer program can include students' IDs as part of their registration information, ensuring that any participation or assessment data can then be examined by subgroup, not just as a single data set. Having this information is essential for determining whether the program is serving those who need it most or whether outcomes vary substantially for different groups of children.

ENSURE COMMUNITY REPRESENTATION ON THE CABINET

Mayors should choose Cabinet members with community representation in mind. As governing bodies that make significant decisions affecting children and families across the community, it is important to have formal, structural representation of the various constituencies making up the community. This means aiming for a Cabinet whose membership reflects the racial composition of the broader community and including organizations on the Cabinet that represent diverse constituencies. Depending on the makeup of municipal and organizational leadership within your community, this may happen naturally; if not, mayors should seek out leaders of color and those whose lived experiences are similar to those the Cabinet's work aims to help.

Another way to broaden the range of voices and perspectives advising the Cabinet and to ensure authentic representation of historically marginalized constituencies—who are those most impacted by the Cabinet's work—is to create a community advisory council. EdRedesign recently developed a concept for such a council, which is a separate body of community members that meets regularly and both advises and has representation on the Cabinet. A community council would help address the challenge many Cabinets face with community engagement and creating political demand for the Cabinet's work, both of which are essential to the Cabinet's sustainability over time. Its membership would include people with both organizational and informal leadership roles within the community. As of this writing, the Chattanooga–Hamilton County Children's Cabinet is considering creating an advisory council whose members broadly reflect the community and who would also have representation on the Cabinet itself.

Minneapolis has taken a youth-focused approach to the community advisory: the city established the Minneapolis Youth Congress in 2007 to advise the Minneapolis Youth Coordinating Board and other youth-serving organizations. Comprised of fifty eighth through twelfth graders, the Youth Congress uses the motto, "No Decision About Us Without Us," meaning that youth should be involved in making important decisions that impact them. The congress focuses on racial equity and learning about government structures. Advisory councils should be assembled in ways that ensure their impact on the Cabinet by having representatives on the Cabinet or a clear expectation to seriously consider the council's recommendations. At their best, these councils are complementary to a Cabinet and add emphasis and depth to perspectives already represented on the Cabinet.

Creating formal working groups with a meaningful role in determining policy can also serve to increase the Cabinet's representation. These groups are generally tasked with developing concrete proposals and, in some cases, overseeing programmatic implementation in a specific content area. They often include one or more Cabinet members along with other experts and community representatives. As we mention in the previous chapter, Denver recently established five subcommittees to its Cabinet intended to "support and advise the full Children's Cabinet on issues impacting Denver children and youth." While each subcommittee's membership must include at least two Cabinet members, they also have the effect of broadening community participation, since the Cabinet itself is structured to include only heads of municipal organizations. The subcommittees provide a way to engage a range of perspectives and experiences beyond those formally on the Cabinet.

ENGAGE FAMILIES

Cabinets should begin their community engagement efforts with the families of children who will be impacted by their new policies and programs. Generally, when people talk about community engagement in decisions about children, what they mean is parent and family engagement with schools. And in the experience of many families, this engagement is perfunctory at best, with schools giving information to parents but not soliciting their input, or assigning parents specific tasks but not engaging them more deeply in their work. While we see community engagement in the work of Children's Cabinets as broader than family engagement with schools, developing strong school-family partnerships is foundational to a broader change in the relationship between institutions and the people they serve. These school and family relationships are particularly critical in the face of the disruptions associated with the pandemic.

Professor Karen Mapp, along with colleague Eyal Bergman at the Harvard Graduate School of Education, developed the latest version of the "Dual Capacity-Building Framework for Family School Partnerships."[6] Designed to improve the partnerships between schools and families, the framework identifies reasons why, historically, these partnerships have not been more effective, while outlining conditions and goals for achieving "effective partnerships that support student and school improvement." Each section of the framework links to resources for strengthening communication and establishing authentic partnership between families and schools.

USE MULTIPLE STRATEGIES TO ENGAGE BROADER COMMUNITIES

Because the business of Children's Cabinets is systems change, strengthening the relationships between schools and families is not enough. Cabinets need to take on a broader effort to learn from multiple constituencies about their vision and priorities for children, to build mechanisms for incorporating this input into the Cabinet's work, and to create a broad consensus across the community for a new commitment to *all* children—whether or not community members have children or are experiencing the challenges the Cabinet aims to address. Before designing solutions for problems that affect certain groups of people more than others, leaders who may not experience those problems themselves should seek to gather the ideas and perspectives of those to be served on both what the solutions should be and how they should be implemented.

Communities and their interests are, of course, not monolithic. Even within particular affinity groups—residents of a specific neighborhood, parents of schoolchildren, those who identify with a particular racial or ethnic group, those who benefit from the status quo—there is not a single viewpoint. Cabinets need to develop a nuanced perception of who makes up their community, to listen to the concerns and ideas of traditionally underrepresented groups, *and* to translate those into meaningful, sustained, two-way interactions.

The first component of community engagement involves taking time for thoughtful, committed outreach by creating opportunities to hear from members of the community. To do this effectively, Cabinet representatives need to ensure that people know about community meetings (or other opportunities for community members to provide input and perspective) and that they are at accessible venues and times, with attention to language accessibility and childcare issues. Cabinet members should develop relationships with leaders of community organizations and religious institutions to help facilitate this process.

Organize Community-wide Summits

Another approach to soliciting meaningful community input on priorities is to engage in an intensive process over a short time through a community-wide summit. The city of Providence took this approach in 2017, hiring a local community organizer and expert in youth participatory action with funding from the Nellie Mae Foundation. Over four hundred students, teachers, families, and other community members participated in the summit, which addressed five priority areas:

- Improving facilities districtwide
- Cultivating culturally responsive learning
- Strengthening diversity and inclusion
- Improving outcomes for English language learners
- Leveraging community partnerships in schools

In breakout sessions for each priority area, summit participants identified short- and long-term goals, such as engaging in an asset-mapping process to determine how resources are being used in Providence to support children and who is providing services. The summit yielded a report and recommendations for action that were shared with the Cabinet and the public, and the Cabinet committed to incorporating the report's findings into its work.

Build Community Participation into Decision-Making

One reason for community distrust of government organizations is the lack of meaningful follow-through on recommendations. If Cabinets want to build trust, they should acknowledge this history and make genuine commitments to incorporating community input into their actions. The strategies we discuss above for creating Cabinets with representative membership and formal advisories are important ways to create meaningful community participation. Cabinets should implement a clear process to address and incorporate community recommendations and to hear regularly from community members in a variety of formats, from large-scale, grassroots-led events to meetings at sites across the community to a family and community advisory group. What is equally important is to build in accountability structures for ensuring input leads to tangible action.

DESIGN INITIATIVES FOR EQUITY

Moving from intention to sustained action is the key to building community trust and creating lasting change. Historically, opportunities have not been equally distributed, with more enrichment programs, health services, high-quality schools, and other services more readily available in more affluent neighborhoods with fewer people of color.

In choosing which initiatives to prioritize and where to locate them, Cabinets should explicitly consider the impact on and value for children of color.

Use a Design-Centered Approach

One strategy for taking action is to incorporate the principles of design thinking into creating a comprehensive strategy. Starting from the premise that current systems are designed for inequity and can be redesigned to combat it, a collaborative of three leaders in equity and design—Caroline Hill, founder of 228 Accelerator; Michelle Molitor, executive director of the Equity Lab; and Christine Ortiz, founder of Equity Meets Design—have created equityXdesign: a "process for antiracist and equitable design, it is guided by three central beliefs: innovation's need for inclusion and intentional design, the indistinguishable relationship between the past and the present, and our moral imperative to live in the future we desire to create."[7] They have developed a free, self-paced introductory course set of publicly available tools and processes for incorporating the dual lenses of racial equity and design thinking into processes for setting goals and taking action.[8]

The equityXdesign strategy is built on three "centering beliefs" that focus on understanding history, inclusion in the process, and seeing the process of design as integral to its product. It also uses five design principles: design at the margins, start with yourself, cede power, make the invisible visible, and speak to the future.

Incorporate Targeted Universalism

Another strategy for addressing equity through collaborative action is "targeted universalism." This approach combines universal goals with interventions targeted to those who need them most and have historically suffered from underinvestment. Targeted universalism avoids some of the stigma attached to interventions that benefit a defined subset of the population as well as some of the pushback from more privileged families who feel they're being excluded from opportunities. At the same time, it enables a focusing of energy and resources where they are most needed. The City Connects strategy for providing integrated student supports is an example of targeted universalism.[9] In this model, a City Connects coordinator creates a profile of each child in a school with input from that child's teacher, outside data, and other information. The coordinator identifies for each child a level of need for support and enrichment, so while every child gets a plan, some plans are more intensive than others.

The key to creating an equity-embedded approach to systems change is a genuine commitment to work on shaping reforms in partnership with those who are most harmed by the existing system. It's time to move away from token measures—in representation, community outreach, funding, data use, and program choices—to a deep restructuring of opportunity that actively works to redress the ways racism and other prejudices have served to reproduce existing distributions of opportunity rather than making it available to all. This equity work must constantly be promoted by leaders as absolutely top priority.

Key Tasks for Embedding Equity and Engaging the Community

- Acknowledge your community's history and current reality
- Name equity as your goal
- Use data as a tool to understand and improve equity
- Ensure community representation on the Cabinet
- Engage families
- Use multiple strategies to engage broader communities
- Design initiatives for equity

CHAPTER 4

Take Strategic Action

The point of any cross-sector collaboration is to effect meaningful, lasting change that benefits children. No amount of data examination, ambitious goals, new relationships, or careful planning will improve children's lives without action. This may seem obvious, but it can be surprisingly easy to get stuck in the system-building and planning stages of the work. The essential role of Cabinets is to identify which actions will enable their communities to reach their goals by developing a plan and executing it. Along the way, Cabinet members need to change people's mindsets and ways of operating, communicate the value of these activities to the public, create structural changes that ensure the long-term sustainability of these actions, and assess whether or not the interventions are making a difference. Carrying out collaborative action is a multistep process requiring sequenced engagement of community, organizations, and government entities.

The scope of Cabinets' work often focuses on strategies that mitigate the effects of poverty and racism in a variety of ways. To the extent possible, Cabinets and the communities they serve should also work to address the root causes of inequity and effect structural changes designed to reduce it. This means advocating for and using governmental authority to impact key policy levers such as housing, school funding and quality, income and wealth inequality, universal access to health care, and so on. The current emphasis within the field of health care on understanding and improving the social determinants of health—the conditions and environments that lead to better or worse health outcomes—has a strong corollary in education. Just as prevention is essential for health, addressing the inequitable contexts in which children and families live is key to achieving success for all.

Taking action involves a number of key stages that we will walk through in this chapter: establish a broad, shared vision; identify an ambitious North Star goal; conduct a gap analysis; select high-impact strategies and specific initiatives; and implement the plan. The order of these steps may vary, though, depending on the way the community has entered into the cross-sector collaboration. If, for example, there has been a precipitating crisis or event that spurred the Cabinet's creation, the North Star goal may already be defined before the Cabinet is even convened. In Tacoma, for example, a news story in *USA Today* identifying the city's high schools as "dropout factories" drove the organizing focus of increasing graduation rates; their cross-sector effort formed specifically to address this overarching goal. Louisville's collaboration formed in response to an established goal of increasing the number of residents with college degrees after a high-profile, business roundtable report challenged the city to upgrade its labor market. In these cases, the gap analysis will inform the steps to reach their goal rather than to define it. In communities that begin this effort from a more generalized sense of urgency about inequitable opportunities and outcomes for children, the gap analysis may point to a specific entry point and focus for the effort.

ESTABLISH A CRADLE-TO-CAREER VISION

Children's Cabinets should start by grounding their efforts in a broad vision that encompasses the entire arc of a child's development, from birth through postsecondary completion. Communities need to take the same perspective parents do with their own children: that every stage is an important passage that deserves particular attention, and raising children isn't over until they reach adulthood with the skills to hold a job, be active community members, and support a family, if they so choose. There are no single, silver-bullet solutions that would enable policy makers to intervene at a certain point in children's lives to ensure success. Even those, like high-quality early childhood education, which have well-researched, long-term benefits will only yield success if followed up with a sequence of subsequent educational interventions that secure the initial gains.

A number of organizations have elaborated their own versions of the stages in a cradle-to-career pipeline, including the Brookings Institute's Human Genome Project, the Forum for Youth Investment, Strive Together, the Harlem Children's Zone, and others. While these models differ in the particular markers used to gauge whether children are on track, they all identify, at a minimum, specific milestones at early childhood, elementary school, secondary school, and postsecondary transition, while recognizing that ensuring children reach these milestones requires a constellation of supports and interventions at each stage. Cabinets should take the time to envision what a cradle-to-career system would look like in their communities and use that as a framework for all of their actions. This makes visible the magnitude and scope of the undertaking and codifies a systemic approach, while also making it easier to see how each specific element of the Cabinet's work is contributing to a bigger, comprehensive vision.

CREATE PERSONALIZED SUPPORTS FOR EACH STUDENT

The theory behind cross-sector collaboration is that by working together, concerned community leaders can build systems of support for children from birth through a successful postsecondary transition. The corollary to this is that we need to support each *individual* child rather than offering a set of generic opportunities and interventions that may or may not be the right ones for any given child. We made the case in the introduction that different children have vastly different and widely inequitable life experiences, assets, challenges, supports, opportunities, and needs, and that our current system fails miserably to address these differences. To overcome this mismatch between current systems and children's needs, EdRedesign has been developing a strategy of individualized success planning customized for each student. This approach, in its most comprehensive form, involves identifying each student's academic and nonacademic strengths, interests, and needs, and developing and implementing a personalized plan for support. Each By All Means community is developing its own version of success planning, ranging from partnering with Boston College–based City Connects to implementing a comprehensive program of personalized supports to developing new databases that link students with social and academic services to cocreating plans with middle school students for a successful transition to high school. Through a cross-sector, collaborative strategy, these communities are creating cradle-to-career education, support, and opportunity systems with an individualized approach tailored to each student. In so doing, these initiatives attack the problems of fragmentation by building a significantly more coherent youth development system that remedies the failure of the one-size-fits-all approach to children. This work includes a focus on both policy and investments. Cabinets must push to replace harmful, inequitable policies with constructive ones designed to build out the services and supports for young people. Inevitably, Cabinets will need to pay attention to budgets and become advocates for increased investments in children. The Cabinet must function to envision, collaborate, and advocate for the changes necessary to build a successful cradle-to-career pipeline serving all students, especially those most disadvantaged by the current system.

IDENTIFY A NORTH STAR GOAL

After creating a vision, the next step is to identify an ambitious North Star goal that can serve as an important focal point. As we discuss above, this aspirational goal may present itself organically as the reason for creating the Cabinet in the first place. If not, the idea is to choose a goal with specific metrics and quantifiable targets as initial measures that will indicate the success of the collaboration.

What we have seen in practice is that cross-sector collaborations generally take one of three approaches to framing their work: they choose an ambitious North Star goal; they identify a broad umbrella under which multiple efforts can fit without defining a specific focus; or they identify a defined area of focus without setting a target outcome. In the first approach, exemplified by Louisville, Chattanooga–Hamilton County, and Tacoma, the community identifies increasing the number of students earning college degrees or other meaningful postsecondary attainment as its ultimate goal. Tacoma's Graduate Tacoma initiative, for example, targeted increasing the high school graduation rate by 50 percent its primary objective, while also tracking and reporting on over a dozen other academic and community-based metrics that serve as important intermediate markers of progress and opportunity. Organizing to achieve a specific goal has enabled Tacoma's leaders to define and focus the work more clearly than would be the case with a more general framing. Having a defined aim also communicates a clear message to the broader community about what the initiative is trying to accomplish and provides an easy rallying cry, while helping people in different agencies and organizations see how they might contribute.

In the second approach, taken by Salem's collaborative initiative, the Children's Cabinet adopted the Our Salem, Our Kids framework to create a sense of shared community-wide responsibility for improving services and outcomes for children. Cabinet members found that having this umbrella helped them understand how the different elements of the effort fit together as part of a unified vision. The third strategy is the one taken by the Illinois Partnership for Resilience. Its collaboration, which operates in two regions of the state, originated as a partnership between educators and medical professionals to address alarming levels of trauma among children. The partnership did not begin with a specific target outcome, but its organizational focus on childhood trauma has led to programs and services that enable practitioners to address the effects of trauma through teacher professional development, implementation of mental health initiatives, provision of health care, and other approaches.

For collaborations like those in Tacoma and Louisville that do choose a North Star, the goal is often successful completion of high school or even postsecondary education or training. This makes sense, since other long-term objectives would stop short of ensuring that students have reached a milestone that puts them on a path to success. And while this framing may seem narrowly academic, in reality it is not. Any academic goal, especially one set at the end of high school or postsecondary education, encompasses a host of nonacademic components across the entire time span from birth on, since so many nonschool factors impact whether or not a child will attain academic success. Cabinets should regularly acknowledge, address, and measure their success in meeting children's out-of-school needs. The North Star should also have value that will be clearly recognized throughout the community and should be ambitious enough to justify the time, effort, and cost.

Along with the long-term, ambitious goal, Cabinets need to identify interim goals aligned with the specific actions they undertake as a way to show the progress the effort is making. One way to highlight progress is through documenting and celebrating quick wins, which are short-term indicators of success. These can include increases to programming and funding in addition to improvements in outcomes.

CONDUCT A GAP ANALYSIS

In the previous chapter, we discussed the importance of grounding collaborative work in an analysis of data to determine the community's most-pressing needs. Before deciding what work to take on first, Cabinets need to use data from multiple sectors to conduct a gap analysis—that is, to identify the gaps between what children need for viable pathways to success and what the community is currently offering. As part of this gap analysis, communities must identify where they are and where they would like to be on a range of outcome measures that includes academic achievement, health, mental health, and other measures of child and community well-being. Disaggregating data by key categories that include economic status, race, language, disability, and geography within the community is essential for equity purposes and to develop an understanding of the profound disparities of opportunities and outcomes between those with privilege and those without.

Along with outcomes data, Cabinets should examine opportunity and access data as well as data on how the community is spending its money. Opportunity and access indicators can include anything from the percent of children in each subgroup with regular access to health care or who attend high-quality preschools or who are suspended from school. Bringing in financial data for programs from different sectors that affect children shows how close the fit is between the community's most-pressing needs and its investments—and can surface patterns of inefficiency or neglect. Sharing data across sectors in these three areas—outcomes, opportunity, and spending—will help identify intersecting areas of need and opportunity. In addition to academic measures at all levels of the school system, the gap analysis should uncover health data, early childhood program participation, measures of mental health and trauma, afterschool and summer opportunities, and possibly even data on housing or justice system involvement. We discuss this further in chapter 5.

USE DATA TO MAKE STRATEGIC DECISIONS ABOUT PROGRAMS AND FUNDING

It's hard to imagine any Cabinet doing more to use data for decision-making than Denver's Children's Cabinet. Under the guidance of a professional geographer, Denver uses a neighborhood-focused analysis of outcomes, needs, programs, and even funding to make important decisions about where to focus its efforts. Its annual Child Well-Being Index includes a wide range of data points, from those measuring education and child development to health and safety (see figure 4.1 for an example). A companion analysis details spending on children, broken down by neighborhood as well as by subgroup. The Cabinet's online interactive maps enable the public to see data broken down by neighborhood on each element of the index.

Examining trends and outcomes, though, will only reveal the current story of how well a community is doing against the greatest areas

FIGURE 4.1 Denver Children's Cabinet 2020 Child Well-Being Index

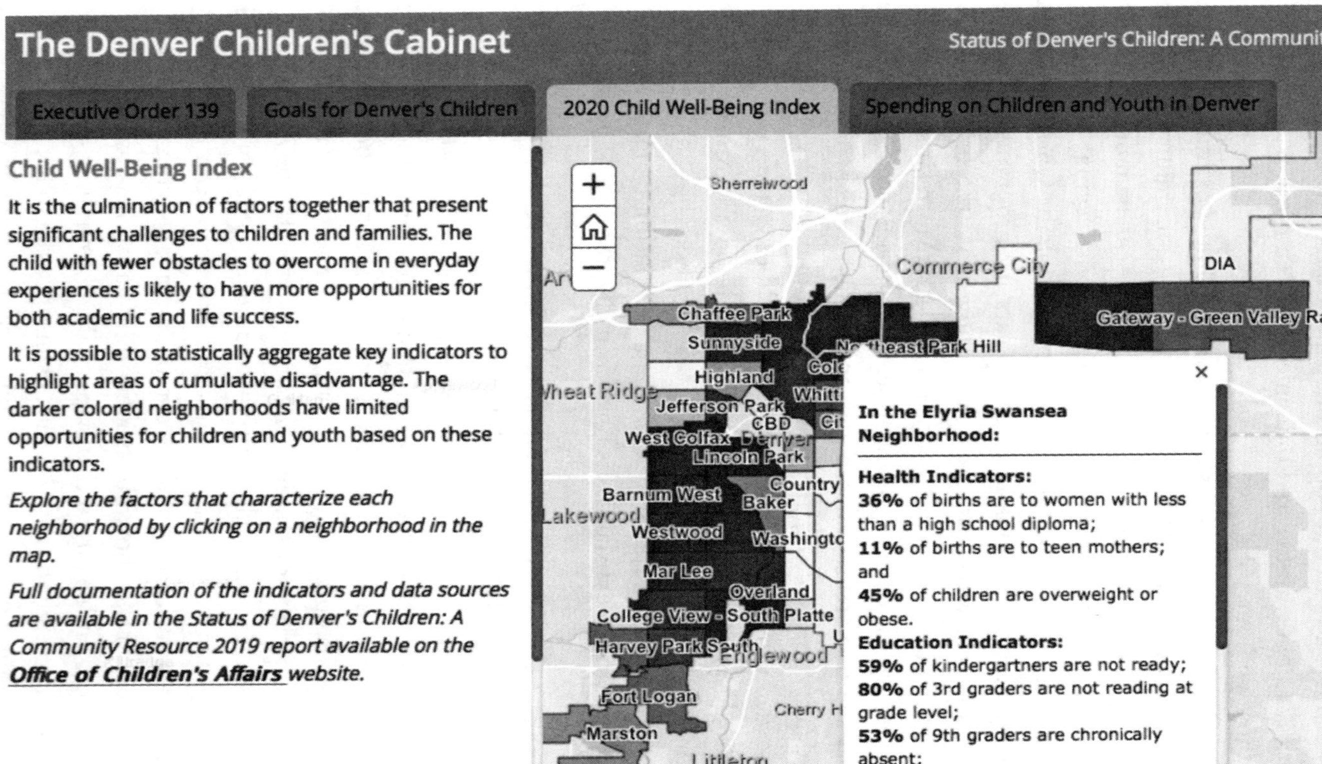

of need; it will not identify specific solutions. Using data to make decisions is important at every stage of cross-sector collaboration, but Cabinets need to take care not to let this data analysis substitute for taking action. Communities should approach the data analysis phase with an action-oriented mindset and a clear timeline and process for moving from information to implementation. Data analysis is a take-off point for action.

In every community, the data will reveal multiple—sometimes seemingly overwhelming—needs and challenges, particularly for the most vulnerable children. Before Cabinets decide what specific actions to take, they should use their analysis of data to identify priority areas of focus and high-impact interventions that will help their communities reach their long-term objectives. From there, Cabinets must decide on a set of intermediate goals, strategies to achieve them, and clear, next steps for implementation. We discuss key considerations for choosing actions below.

SELECT HIGH-IMPACT, SUSTAINABLE STRATEGIES AND ACTIONS

All the preceding steps still do not lead automatically to a specific strategic point of entry for a community's work. It takes skillful leadership and committed collaboration to navigate the transition from setting goals to taking action. If a community's objective is to increase the number of college graduates or the percent of students graduating from high school, for example, everything from early childhood education to improved access to medical care to college Promise Scholarships could be reasonable points of entry and interventions.

Strategy selection is a crucial and complex task for Cabinets, which must weigh practical, financial, and political considerations in addition to research-based evidence of the value of that strategy. Communities should undertake a decision-making process that examines the data about the community's biggest challenges while investigating the research on strategies that have worked elsewhere. The process should also take into account which courses of action are most feasible on a number of dimensions. Successful actions are ones that have champions, can build momentum, are fundable, are likely to be embraced by those responsible for implementation, and will yield meaningful changes for children.

Align Actions with a Theory of Change

A theory of change is simply an articulation of anticipated cause and effect: "if we do *x*, we expect *y* to result." The collective impact principle of creating shared goals as the foundation of cross-sector collaboration is focused on the *y*, or what the collective group wants to achieve. This may sound technical, but it's really about the vision for the work and how to achieve it. It can be surprisingly easy to embrace particular actions without making explicit their expected value or how they contribute toward reaching the cross-sector collaborative's long-term goals.

Choose High-Value Interventions

Cross-sector collaborations have gravitated toward a handful of action areas. These include early childhood learning, health, social-emotional well-being, chronic absenteeism, connecting children with integrated supports and social services, and out-of-school opportunities. For some of these areas, the impact on children's development and success is well established. Ample research on early childhood, for example, has made abundantly clear the importance of this time period for lifelong well-being, academic achievement, and success on a wide range of measures. Recent research has shown the impact of early brain development on a person's life trajectory as well as vividly illustrating the economic value of early intervention. Expanding access to high-quality preK programs has become a popular choice for this reason, enjoying broad social support and a relatively robust set of funding opportunities. Somerville is one of the By All Means communities that have made early childhood education a priority. The city has been able to substantially increase its preschool programming after getting grants of about $3 million in combined state and private funding.

Other areas, such as social-emotional well-being, are still building an evidence and experience base as well as a critical mass of support for specific interventions, although among those who work with children, the need for action on this front is well established. When EdRedesign formed the By All Means consortium, the most consistently identified challenge named by superintendents was the rising need for mental health support. Children are facing a mental health crisis, and schools see this firsthand every day. Providence has prioritized children's mental health by expanding the number of counselors in schools and hiring a mental health coordinator for the school district. In addition, the two By All Means sites in Illinois were founded out of a commitment to creating cross-sector strategies for addressing childhood trauma.

Identify Champions of the Work

Implementing new initiatives is time-consuming and demanding work. There need to be people willing to take the lead in defining the scope, finding funding, communicating the vision, and developing a concrete plan for implementation. Some of this can occur at the Cabinet level, but generally a smaller working group takes responsibility for fleshing out and enacting specific initiatives. Champions essentially serve as visible, forceful advocates and cheerleaders for the effort, bringing the enthusiasm and energy needed to get a project underway and then helping to sustain its momentum. Champions can be found in all corners of the community by looking for trusted, recognized leaders in government; community-based, neighborhood, and civic organizations; business; unions; grassroots and advocacy groups; philanthropies; educational institutions; or a host of other community initiatives. What's most important is that the champion be a highly respected leader with access and influence, high levels of integrity, and the belief, energy, and capacity to focus on the Cabinet's particular initiative.

Develop a Funding Plan

Determining whether there are funding sources for an initiative is a key step in deciding whether or not it is viable, and Cabinets should consider the likelihood of finding funding before going too far down any particular programmatic path. Costs vary widely depending on the scope and scale of the activity, but could include a wide range of needs, including program staff, capital costs, training, college scholarships, and program evaluation. Funding for staff positions to implement and oversee programs is also important to their success. Potential sources of funding include Cabinet members committing the money from their existing organizational budgets; raising outside funds from businesses, individuals, philanthropies, and government grants at federal and state levels; or even undertaking a ballot proposal to raise dedicated local revenue. Some communities have also found other funding sources, such as Salem's use of its local community hospital's payment in lieu of taxes commitment to fund its partnership with City Connects.

Build Support for Implementation

Moving from Cabinet-level identification of initiatives to on-the-ground implementation can easily be a disconnected process without Cabinet leaders doing important engagement work to involve programmatic staff and key community leaders in shaping the effort. If the Cabinet has a backbone organization, it should be central in guiding the work and engaging partners and participants. Cabinet working groups can form a useful bridge between the Cabinet and the programs that will directly impact children. If a Cabinet chooses, for example, to focus on chronic absenteeism through a combination of programs to improve children's health, address transportation challenges, and create a school-based messaging campaign, it is important for everyone involved to understand not just whatever new actions they'll be taking, but how these actions fit into the Cabinet's larger vision for youth and, thus, contribute to the achievement of a shared goal. If existing staff are being asked to substantially change the way they operate, then the leaders must bring them into the planning and address their concerns. Only in this way will their buy-in be assured.

Identify Each Organization's Role

While North Star goals can sound entirely aspirational in nature, achieving them requires the work of multiple partners at a wide range of points of intervention. The rationale for cross-sector collaboration is the inability of any single sector to solve complex social problems. If the goal is to ensure youth reach much higher rates of secondary or postsecondary achievement, the solution lies in taking a multipronged approach to accomplishing this. It takes, as the saying goes, a whole village. The value of working collaboratively is in combining forces, integrating action, and assuming collective rather than individual responsibility for achieving the goal of children's success and well-being. Everyone at the table has something important to contribute, and this involvement will keep people engaged, accountable, and present at meetings to stay informed and active in shaping the work.

For Children's Cabinets, identifying who will take which role can be one of the more politically challenging elements of cross-sector work. For example, when role assignments, such as a new position to coordinate afterschool programming or additional mental health counselors in schools, come with dedicated financial resources, competition for scarce resources can emerge and become problematic, requiring sensitive negotiations. Conversely, some Cabinet members may be reluctant to take on new organizational responsibilities or to change their cultures. While Cabinets are designed to help communities work across sectors and move from siloed to collaborative actions, achieving that requires substantial change in the way participating organizations currently do business.

Schools are generally presumed to have the primary responsibility for children's well-being (even though they seldom have the resources and capacity to fulfill this responsibility), and this is not likely to change in the near future. They should and do have a central role in Children's Cabinets and often in implementing the work the Cabinets identify. However, the point of the Cabinets is to share the responsibility for children's well-being because schools as typically designed, staffed, and resourced lack sufficient capacity to ensure children's well-being. Consequently, Cabinets view this work as a community responsibility rather than just an expectation of the schools. The existence of the Cabinet acknowledges that schools should not and cannot be expected to carry the full burden of meeting children's needs. Determining what should happen within schools, what should be accomplished in partnership with schools, and what should be externally provided but complementary is an important part of any Cabinet's work in preparing for implementation.

Some sectors represented at Cabinet tables typically have limited, if any, experience in coordinating with the schools. Their participation in the Cabinet, however, will likely necessitate significant collaboration with the school system. For example, there may be more formal partnerships between the out-of-school, social services, and health sectors with the schools. Cabinet leaders must negotiate these partnerships, paying attention to details such as who will take which roles in these newly conceived partnerships. The superintendent's participation in all of this work is crucial.

Structurally, creating organizational working groups is an effective way to engage a broader set of constituents in specific elements of the action, and most Cabinets choose this route. Somerville established working groups at its Cabinet's inception focused on expanding health, early childhood, and out-of-school opportunities that carried out deeper planning and implementation efforts. Denver also recently formed working groups to develop strategies for data, policy, innovation, budget, and a child safety net, and these groups also serve as a way to engage a broader set of organizations and community representatives than is possible on the Cabinet itself, which includes only municipal agencies.

Partner with Organizations That Have Programmatic Models

One way to accelerate action is to partner with an existing organization that has an established program model in an area your community has identified as a priority. The advantage of doing this is getting a complete, thoroughly considered design and the ability to implement it more quickly than if you develop a program from scratch. These partnerships can offer a variety of advantages including a theory of change for the intervention, operational practices, technical assistance, and professional development, as well as data and evaluation support.

Among the By All Means communities, for example, both Salem and Chattanooga–Hamilton County opted to partner with City Connects to implement their model for integrated student support. City Connects, which is based at Boston College, has a decades-long track record of implementing schoolwide programs to support individual students. In City Connects schools, a coordinator works with teachers to develop a comprehensive assessment of each student's needs, interests, and strengths. It is also the coordinator's job to develop and implement a plan for supporting each child through connections to academic and other services. The City Connects research team collects data on everything from fidelity of implementation to the number and type of services provided, and following several years of implementation, on student academic outcomes as well.

Afterschool programming is another area in which partnering with established program models can speed implementation. In fact, some By All Means communities brought in several different providers with distinct models and cultures to meet different needs for out-of-school time. Somerville, for example, affiliated with three different programs to meet its goal of creating a new systemic approach to providing afterschool programming to middle school students. One of these, Breakthrough Greater Boston, brought its well-established national model for middle school summer and school-year programming to Somerville. Using near-peer college students as teachers, Breakthrough builds student self-efficacy, college focus, and social-emotional skills through a vibrant group culture. Another partner in Somerville is the Calculus Project, which focuses on developing the math skills of middle school students of color to prepare them to take high-level math classes in high school. It, too, has an established national presence. The city designated funding for a city staff position to coordinate afterschool programming and these partnerships, creating a coherent system in place of the previous patchwork of options.

Bringing in a fully formed model does come with some caveats, though. Programs developed externally may garner less buy-in than those developed in partnership with members of the community, particularly if the decision is made without broad-based input. The cultures and goals of different organizations can also be different, leading to implementation challenges. Partnerships may also come with costs beyond those to operate the program, which can be hard to fund within tight budgets. Sometimes, too, outside organizations may simply misunderstand important aspects of the local context. As an example, Say Yes to Education intended to bring its college scholarship and student support model to Louisville. The Say Yes model removes financial barriers to postsecondary education for all graduating students within a school district by raising funds to provide college scholarships that fill the gap between financial aid and the cost of attendance. In previous Say Yes districts, most students had qualified for substantial financial aid, reducing the amount of the gap for each student. In greater Louisville's suburban-urban Jefferson County School District, though, many students did not qualify for large amounts of financial aid, making the amount of money that needed to be raised for the scholarship program more than three times greater than Say Yes had originally anticipated. This discrepancy proved too great to overcome. While Louisville did continue its partnership with Say Yes in a different form and continues to pursue key elements of its theory of action, the partnership was much more limited than Louisville had initially expected.

Codevelop Initiatives with Outside Partners

An alternative to bringing in a fully developed program is to codevelop an initiative with one or more partners. This can take more time and involves more design work, but it also retains more local autonomy and allows for a greater degree of local customization. In Louisville, for example, the Cabinet has partnered with the data platform Unite Us to develop a customized platform to streamline children's referrals to social services. When Louisville's Cabinet decided it needed a data platform to connect school and social services data to better serve individual students, it created a subcommittee to consider and vet several options. Headed by the CEO of Louisville's Metro United Way, the committee ultimately chose the Unite Us platform, in part because of the company's willingness to work as a partner with Louisville to design a version tailored to Louisville's needs.

Originally created as a way to streamline supports addressing the social determinants of health, Unite Us takes "a mission-driven approach to redefining the way health is delivered across communities."

Unite Us worked closely with the Metro United Way and Jefferson County Public Schools to identify the components to include in Louisville's platform and to create data-sharing agreements and data security protocols. The social services component of the platform is currently operating, and they are in the process of expanding this to the school system as well. When that is in place, a defined number of school staff will have licenses to access the platform and will be trained in its use. While Unite Us was originally intended to be rolled out in the school system in the fall of 2020, school closures due to Covid-19 have delayed that until the winter of 2021.

Build a Homegrown Effort

Another programmatic approach is to develop the intervention internally, although even this often involves forming partnerships given the cross-sector nature of this work. Illinois's Partnership for Resilience, for example, is organized to address the goal of reducing childhood trauma. To do this, it has created partnerships between schools and health providers, with substantial community input. Its work has taken a number of forms, including training hundreds of teachers in trauma-informed practices and providing dental and vision care directly to children through mobile vans. The advantages of this approach include a more participatory planning process, tight alignment between local goals and actions, and avoiding the costs of partnership. One challenge is that this strategy may require a greater time commitment for planning and implementation without the proven success model available through other programs.

KEEP A SYSTEMS FOCUS WHILE TAKING CONCRETE ACTIONS

As the Cabinets move from vision to action, they—and also importantly, their backbone organizations—must sustain a commitment to their ambitious long-term visions as well as the commitment to take a series of near-term, tangible actions. While these actions may feel, initially, much more limited than the sweeping systems change to which the Cabinets aspire, seeing each specific initiative as a piece in the full cradle-to-career pipeline can help cross-sector collaborations understand how they are building toward a complete system. There is no quick fix or silver-bullet intervention to meet the complex challenges Cabinets are working to address. Leaders must publicly and privately acknowledge this, at the outset and regularly along the way. They must be clear that this will often be incremental work and will take years to come to fruition. These same leaders must lead the celebration of successes along the way and the nurturance of hope and confidence in the achievement of the ultimate goals. In the end, though, the work begins with taking active steps in the direction of building new, more effective and equitable systems of developing and educating our children. The "bias toward action" is a common and laudable characteristic of highly effective Children's Cabinets.

Key Tasks for Taking Strategic Action

- Establish a cradle-to-career vision
- Identify a North Star goal
- Conduct a gap analysis
- Use data to make strategic decisions about programs and funding
- Select high-impact strategies and actions
- Keep a systems focus while taking concrete actions

CHAPTER 5

Utilize Data and Measure Progress

The increasing use of data is one of the most significant changes in education since the onset of school reform. This trend began with the implementation of standards-based school reforms at the state level and culminated with the No Child Left Behind Act (2001) instituting a requirement for schools, districts, and states to collect and publicly report data, disaggregated by demographic subgroup, on student enrollment and achievement. While states had been gathering data on student performance (and some had been disaggregating those data) for nearly a decade beforehand, the new requirement for reporting by race, poverty, gender, disability, and English learner status shined a spotlight on stark average differences in achievement between students in different demographic categories. The publicly reported data made it impossible to ignore that education was not acting as an equalizer. Even in the highest-achieving districts, schools were replicating patterns of inequity. Quantifying these disparities continues to be an important mechanism to support greater equity for children, in schools and beyond.

In the education sector, data serve multiple purposes: to understand children's mastery of content; to diagnose problems for accountability purposes; to administer programing more efficiently; and to communicate transparently with the public. Other sectors, such as early childhood, afterschool and summer programming, and social services have also been strengthening their use of data. For collaborative action initiatives, data and metrics can and should be powerful tools at every stage of the work, from assessing assets, measuring achievement and services, identifying challenges, and setting an agenda to evaluating impact on improving opportunities and supports for children. Metrics also play a key role in enabling different stakeholders to coalesce around a shared agenda and helping them identify the contributions each one can make.

Using data well in collaborative action has proven to be a difficult task, however. There is a tendency to focus on data as an end in itself that is disconnected from actions that will change the outcomes. When data are used well, there is a positive feedback loop between goals, data, and action. Often, though, there are disconnects that break this loop for a variety of reasons. For example, mayors, superintendents, and other agency heads may be reluctant to set specific ambitious target outcomes, since a failure to reach them would damage their credibility and political capital.

The intent of this chapter is to describe the interconnectedness of goals, actions, data, and metrics and to offer a framework for their effective use in collaborative action initiatives. We lay out a playbook of best practices for Children's Cabinets for the use of data and metrics at all stages of their work—from conducting a gap analysis and establishing a Children's Cabinet to identifying an aligned set of metrics and strategies to measuring targeted outcomes. This playbook is grounded in the Measures of Success framework we created and continue to refine in collaboration with our By All Means communities, based on their need for a set of measurement tools that capture the macro elements ranging from the development of committed leadership to the raising of sustainable funding to the micro program evaluation elements such as access to and quality of services.

CONDUCT A GAP ANALYSIS

One of the first tasks of a collaborative action initiative is to examine data from across the community to better understand needs, challenges, and opportunities. By the time leaders in a community decide to act collaboratively and create a Children's Cabinet, they have usually already identified a challenge that feels urgent enough to spur structural changes to the way they have been attending to the development and education of children. Their understanding of the problem is undoubtedly rooted in data, at least loosely: graduation rates may be alarming, or teen suicide may have spiked in recent years, or a high percentage of jobs may be going unfilled because of a mismatch in skills between the jobs and the local workforce. A community may define the focused problem as a single issue or as a constellation of challenges under a broader framework.

Once the Children's Cabinet is constituted, though, it should pause before setting concrete goals or choosing areas of focus to ground its actions in a solid understanding of data. To do this, the Cabinet should conduct a deeper gap analysis that identifies the difference between where the community is and where it strives to be on a number of dimensions. In other words, the Cabinet needs to dig deeper to determine not just the extent of a gap or problem but the cause of the gap. Once identified, that cause serves as the center of a theory of the problem that, in turn, leads to analysis to determine a point of entry for remedying the situation and a theory of action for dealing with it.

In such a process, comparing local numbers against the data of other communities, similar regions, states, or the country can provide a sense of where the community may be doing better or worse than the averages elsewhere and can help pinpoint areas for action. This can also help create a more concrete sense of urgency for the Cabinet's work, since the findings of the analysis are likely to yield some surprising and urgent revelations about challenges facing children in the community. For example, the Poughkeepsie Children's Cabinet examined data related to city and school demographics, housing, safety, health, academic outcomes, and economic stability in comparison to the county and state at the outset of its work as a way to more deeply understand the condition of the city. An excerpt of this analysis is shown in figure 5.1.

This gap analysis should include an assessment of the community's assets—the opportunities and supports currently available for children and youth and the areas in which children are succeeding—as well as an analysis of shortcomings. The goal is to use relevant data from a range of sectors to determine areas of greatest need, so the Cabinet can then identify interventions likely to make the most difference. This is not just a technical exercise, but one involving important questions to interrogate through examination of the data: In what areas are there the biggest disparities between subgroups of students? Where do we see improvements over time? Where have we been making investments, and what has been the effect? What is surprising about the data? Do the data from different sectors tell the same story, and do they point to potential solutions?

Another important element of this gap analysis is identifying the status of the community's existing data use and ways it can strengthen its data capacity. Cabinet leaders should assess what additional data are needed, what, if any, data sharing agreements are currently operating in the community, and what other sharing arrangements might be needed. This initial phase can be quick or lengthy, depending on the community's goals, resources, and culture of collaboration. The trick is to find the sweet spot between choosing interventions too quickly before sufficiently understanding the nature of the problem and spending so much time exploring the data that action stalls and the effort loses momentum. There are a few strategies communities can use to help ensure the success of the gap analysis. We provide a sample template to organize your gap analysis in figure 5.2.

FIGURE 5.1 Poughkeepsie Children's Cabinet: Data for decision-making

EXCERPT

Description: As a part of our efforts to establish Executive Committee priorities in the upcoming academic year, we are working to compile relevant children, youth and families data to inform cabinet decision-making. Below we provide key data points on the City of Poughkeepsie's challenges and opportunities in public education and community development.

I. Poverty and Income

- 20.2% of the population lives below the poverty line vs. 11% in New York State (NYS), including 24% of African-Americans (vs. 16% in Dutchess County) and 25% of Hispanics (vs. 15% in Dutchess County)[1]
- 26% of children living in poverty compared to 12% in Dutchess County.[2] 36% of Hispanic children living in poverty vs. 26% of African American vs. 20% of White
- $42,296 median income as compared to $78,028 in Dutchess County and $68,465 in NYS[3]
- $37,354 median income of African-Amercians ($50,765 in Dutchess County) vs. $36,794 of Hispanics ($63,255 in Dutchess County) vs. $49,926 of Whites ($81,130 in Dutchess County)[4]
- 12% of Seniors living in poverty vs. 6% in Dutchess County[5]
- Economically disadvantaged students 73% in Poughkeepsie, compared to 38% in Dutchess County[6]

IV. Health

- 9.5% Low birthweight babies compared to 8.1% in Dutchess County and 7.7% in NYS.[7]
- 6.8% teenage pregnancy rate compared to 1.6% in Dutchess County.[8]
- Food Insecurity: Dutchess County's 2017 food insecurity rate (2017) was 8.6% overall and 14.5% for children, compared to NYS 11.4% overall and 17.6% child[9]

V. Public Safety

- 71 violent crimes per 10,000 residents vs. 18 in Dutchess County and 20 in NYS.[10]
- 91 reports of domestic violence per 10,000 residents vs. 31 in Dutchess County[11]
- Dutchess County rate of childhood abuse and neglect (rate is per 1,000 children under 18) is 17 in 2017, compared to 9 in the U.S.[12]

[1]https://mhvcommunityprofiles.org/financial-stability/people-living-in-poverty-by-race-ethnicity
[2]https://mhvcommunityprofiles.org/children%20and%20youth/children-living-in-poverty
[3]https://mhvcommunityprofiles.org/financial%20stability/median-household-income
[4]https://mhvcommunityprofiles.org/financial-stability/median-household-income-by-race-ethnicity
[5]https://mhvcommunityprofiles.org/financial%20stability/seniors-living-in-poverty
[6]https://mhvcommunityprofiles.org/financial_stability/economically-disadvantaged-students
[7]https://mhvcommunityprofiles.org/health/babies-with-low-birth-weights
[8]https://mhvcommunityprofiles.org/children%20and%20youth/teen-pregnancy
[9]https://www.healthquest.org/Uploads/Public/Documents/Patient-Resources/FINAL_Mid-Hudson%20Regional%20Community%20Health%20Assessment%202019-2021.pdf
[10]https://mhvcommunityprofiles.org/public%20safety/violent-crimes
[11]https://mhvcommunityprofiles.org/public%20safety/domestic-violence
[12]https://mhvcommunityprofiles.org/children_youth/rate-of-child-abuse-and-neglect

FIGURE 5.2 Cross-sector gap analysis template

KEY DATA POINTS BY SECTOR Disaggregated by race/ethnicity, poverty status, disability and ELL status	
Early childhood	· Born at a healthy birthweight · Enrolled in preschool · Meets kindergarten readiness standards
K-12	· Third-grade reading proficiency · Fifth-grade math proficiency · Measure of social-emotional wellbeing/school engagement · Dropout rate · Attendance/chronic absenteeism · Suspension rate · Graduation rate
Higher ed	· Enrolls in higher education · Enrolls in post-secondary training program · Graduates from higher education · Attains a post-secondary certificate
Health and mental health	· Regular doctor visits/primary medical home · Asthma rate · Obesity rate · Regular access to dental care · Rates of depression · Access to mental health provider · Incidence of trauma
Juvenile justice	· Incarcerated youth
Enrichment	· Availability of afterschool and summer programming · Percent of children enrolled
Housing and economic security	· Homeless rate · Housing insecurity rate · Food insecurity rate
Technology	· Percent of children with Internet access
Other	·
What data points are of particular concern?	
What initiatives do we already have underway to address them?	
What are areas we could particularly impact through cross-sector collaboration?	

Start with Student Data

State and local student data systems are gold mines of data and the single best source for information about children of school age. These data systems have been steadily expanding the indicators they collect to include chronic absenteeism, behavior measures such as suspensions, school climate surveys, and other useful metrics. The state or local education agency's website is often the easiest place to find a rich set of data on student demographic characteristics and achievement. These figures are typically available by district and for multiple years, enabling the Cabinet to examine trends over time and by subgroup.

Use Data from Multiple Sources and Agencies

While school data are generally the best starting point because of their breadth and availability, they should not be the only source of data at any stage of the work. Cabinet members representing the health, social services, and other sectors also have important data that can help create a more robust and nuanced picture of how children are doing in the community. Each sector with relevant data should bring them to the gap analysis process in order to enable the Cabinet to see areas of intersecting need and opportunity.

Look at Subgroup Data

Disaggregating data by race, poverty status, disability, gender, and language learner categories is essential for addressing equity, and findings from doing this can be surprising. Disproportionality occurs across sectors, and understanding its nature and extent should be a key driver of interventions. In Oakland, for example, an analysis of kindergarten readiness by subgroup yielded shocking findings about the extent to which Black boys were starting school at much lower rates of preparedness than other children—a fact that has served as a rallying point for intervention.

Define the Parameters and Time Period for the Gap Analysis

While conducting a gap analysis is an important step, spending too much time exploring data can bring the early energy and enthusiasm of starting a Cabinet to a halt. In general, one or two Cabinet sessions should be enough to get a foundational understanding of the data from different sectors. Cabinets should identify in advance the questions they want answered with data and what data they want to see, then set a timeline for the process, review the data as a group, and move ahead with the work.

OPPORTUNITY, EQUITY, AND DATA

In the education sector, we tend to focus narrowly on student outcome data, which report the results of student performance on various academic performance measures, such as grades, promotions to the next grade, and standardized tests. These data are easy to identify and collect, and are readily understandable to the public. However, we know from research and common sense that educational achievement and attainment are directly related to, and usually a function of, the opportunity to learn, as well as other nonacademic factors. As equity is central to the mission of Children's Cabinets, a focus on opportunities to learn, such as access to early education and afterschool and summer enrichment is essential. Identifying the gaps in opportunities for children of various backgrounds to learn challenging academic material or attend high-quality preschools, for example, is critical if Cabinets are to accurately design interventions that will make a difference. If students of color are not performing at high levels on Advanced Placement tests in biology, then the Cabinet's gap analysis should look at whether or not these students have had adequate instruction and laboratory experience in biology to enable them to enter into AP Bio courses, let alone succeed at them. Opportunity is an absolutely core indicator for Cabinets in their work generally and in their efforts to do gap analyses in their communities.

CHOOSE METRICS THAT WILL SUSTAIN COLLABORATIVE ACTION

The metrics communities choose for their initiatives serve several functions: they define the shared goals of the effort and help partners see what they can contribute to achieving them; they provide a way of tracking the initiative's effectiveness and identifying whether changes are needed; and they offer leaders who have put their political capital into this work a way to communicate its value and importance. Because of this, it is important for communities to choose their metrics carefully.

In a recent paper on developing metrics for collaborative action, we propose a set of criteria for communities to use in choosing metrics that will sustain their collaborative action.[1] These criteria, summarized below, synthesize elements of other frameworks for identifying goals and metrics, notably those of the results-based accountability approach and the widely known SMART (specific, measurable, achievable, realistic, and timely) goals. Our criteria focus on elements that will support the effort's sustainability as well as those that evidence suggests will have a meaningful impact on long-term goals for children: a purposeful link to goals, data feasibility, achievable impact, an evidence base, and public resonance.

Choose Metrics the Initiative Can Impact

There can often be a mismatch between the metrics a Cabinet wants to track and the interventions it undertakes. Metrics should align with the Cabinet's theory of action by linking goals with actions. The key question to ask is whether the actions the Cabinet is taking can be expected to change a given outcome and, if so, to what extent and in what time frame.

In considering which metrics to choose, the Cabinet should also look beyond just academic measures to a broader conception of what well-being and success entail. Cabinets should include measures of health, trauma, absenteeism, social-emotional well-being, and other metrics that align with the interventions it is undertaking.

Ensure the Feasibility of Collecting Data

Not all measures the Cabinet would like to use are readily available. This could be because the community has not yet put in place a process for measuring, for example, social and emotional well-being, or because there are barriers to sharing sensitive data such as birth weight data. There are also other practical considerations involved in data collection, including how time consuming, difficult, costly, or politically sensitive particular indicators may be. We discuss data sharing later in this chapter, but it might not always be worth the time and effort needed to reach data sharing agreements for a specific measure. The Cabinet should consider how valuable a measure is and whether there are viable alternatives before deciding whether to collect new data.

Link Metrics with Goals

Metrics provide a way to measure progress toward goals. An important consideration is whether improvement on a given metric contributes to the achievement of the goals of the cross-sector collaboration. Without asking this, it can be surprisingly easy to track data that fall outside the scope of the interventions, which means that there is no reason to expect that improving outcomes for such a measure is an indication that the cross-sector collaboration is having a positive impact. For example, one community initially identified improvement on statewide assessments as a target metric even though its initiatives were focused on grades that are not tested.

Understand the Importance of Public Resonance

One of the more overlooked values of metrics is their usefulness in communicating progress to the public. This is particularly important for mayors, superintendents, and other leaders who are devoting their political capital, money, and time to making big, structural changes that can take years. Making progress on metrics that feel meaningful to the public can go a long way toward justifying the various costs of the initiative and keeping top leadership involved by providing them with evidence of concrete, signature achievements that define their leadership tenure.

Developing a strategy for communicating progress on the metrics is also important. The communities that use metrics most effectively are those that raise the visibility of their metrics in multiple ways, via websites and annual reports, and that make public reporting central to their work. The Graduate Tacoma collaboration, for example, publishes its progress on eighteen student and community metrics each year in a colorful, high-impact book. The metrics serve as a focal point for agencies and backbone staff, giving everyone a common language for what progress looks like and a common understanding of where the effort is making progress and where it is still falling short. The metrics are:

Student indicators

- Quality preschool
- Ready for kindergarten
- Grade 3 reading
- Grade 6 achievement
- Grade 8 math
- Grade 9 achievement
- College entrance exams
- Four-year graduation
- Five-year graduation
- College enrollment
- College completion

Community indicators

- High expectations
- Student attendance
- Parent and family engagement
- Social and emotional support
- Safe and healthy environments
- Out-of-school and summer learning

USE A MEASUREMENT FRAMEWORK THAT CAPTURES THE SCOPE OF THE UNDERTAKING

The ultimate test of an intervention is whether it accomplishes what it sets out to do. For initiatives whose goals are to improve children's current lives and future chances for success and well-being, the key question is whether children do better on meaningful metrics, both academic and nonacademic, than they would have otherwise or, at least, than they had been doing before the intervention. If an initiative is programmatic—meaning that it is a defined, consistent, and specific intervention—it is relatively easy to identify measures and determine whether or not children are doing better on them over time. Tracking the progress and impact of collaborative action generally requires a broader method of capturing the different stages of the work, since the effort includes changes to systems, structures, and ways of doing business that do not lend themselves readily to quantitative analysis. In its early stages, the focus of collaborative action is on creating an organizational structure such as a Children's Cabinet, engaging the community, building public will, defining the focus of the effort, and raising money. These are crucial, foundational undertakings, but they do not immediately yield changes to outcomes for children.

To better reflect the full scope of a cross-sector collaborative's effort, EdRedesign created the Measures of Success framework. This framework includes five categories for tracking the progress of collaborative action initiatives: committed leadership, investment and sustainability, collaborative action, access to services, and child/youth impact (see figure 5.3). The Measures of Success framework is designed to enable Cabinets to clarify their goals and measure their progress at all stages of the process. The first two categories, committed leadership and investment and sustainability, are tracked using rubrics (tables 5.1 and 5.2) for Cabinets to assess where they are on a continuum of development. These elements are essential for creating the conditions and structures for cross-sector collaboration to succeed and include, among other things, shared decision-making, fundraising, and collaborative relationships. The other three categories distill the initiative's theory of change by linking actions with improved opportunities and outcomes. For the Measures of Success to be an effective tool, Cabinets need to recognize the value of regular measurement, feel local ownership of the process and the specific metrics, and commit to regularly reviewing them and using them as a central component of the effort.

Determine Who Will Be Responsible for Coordinating the Measures

Responsibility for collecting data and sharing the metrics needs to be an explicit part of someone's job. For the By All Means communities, the Cabinet coordinator has generally been the one responsible for coordinating the measures at the outset, with that function transitioning to the backbone organization director as backbone structures are more formally established. The measures lead is just the facilitator, though. Getting the full Cabinet to feel committed to using a set of metrics as a core element of its work requires having Cabinet members involved in the process of identifying the relevant metrics, understanding their role in achieving progress, and developing the regular practice of reviewing them.

FIGURE 5.3 The Measures of Success framework

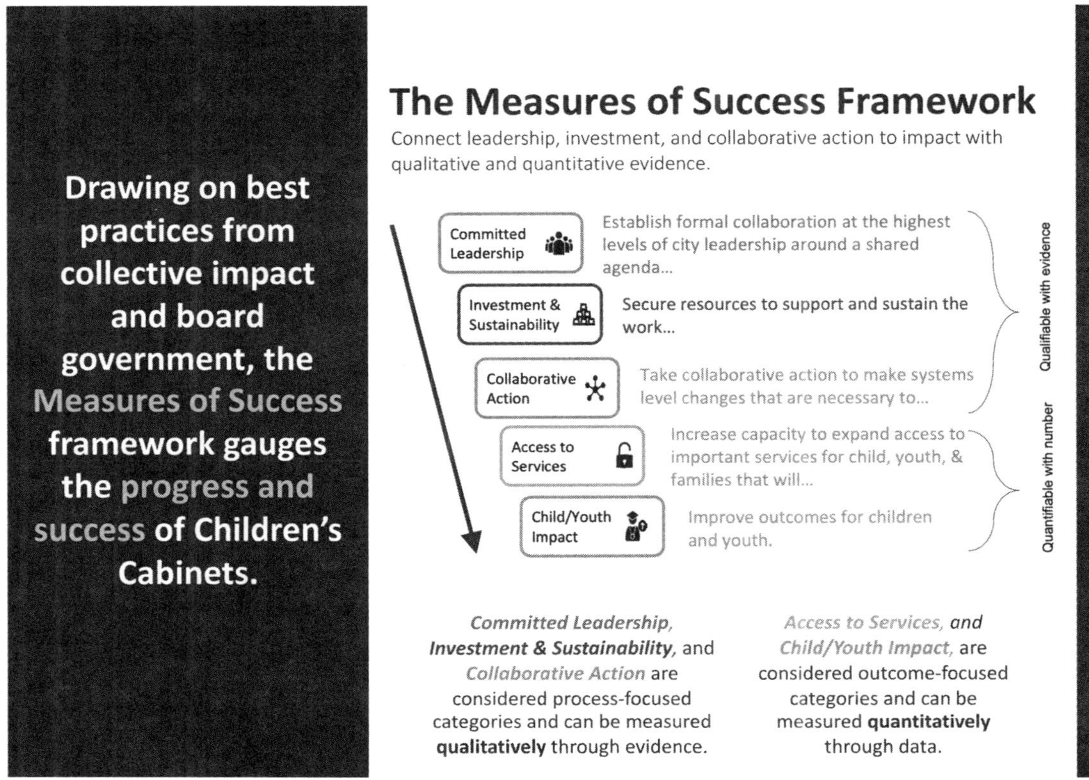

TABLE 5.1 Committed leadership rubric

INSTRUCTIONS: Highlight the stage that best represents your community. In the "Evidence" box, provide bullet-level evidence of that determination.

	Establishing . . .	. . . and Developing . . .	. . . and Mature	Evidence	Next Steps
Governance	Cabinet, including executives from critical agencies and organizations serving children, youth and families, has been formally established, including through MOUs.	Members' roles, obligations, and planned contributions to the work are clearly articulated.	Formalized meeting processes foster participation, discussion, and decision-making.	· · ·	· · ·
Vision	Cabinet has articulated a shared vision that frames, bounds, and communicates its purpose and agenda.	Cabinet has published a report to the community that articulates the shared vision and agenda, along with measurable goals and focused strategies.	Cabinet has published updates to the community, including a public-facing dashboard documenting progress toward goals.	· · ·	· · ·
Operations	Cabinet meetings are scheduled in advance and well-attended by the Mayor, Superintendent, and other critical agency/organization leaders (or senior proxies).	Cabinet meetings are clearly structured, well-facilitated, and productive.	Established communication mechanisms facilitate coordination, collaboration, and progress between Cabinet meetings.	· · ·	· · ·

	Establishing . . .	. . . and Developing . . .	. . . and Mature	Evidence	Next Steps
Data	Cabinet has identified indicators, baselines, and targets for each child-facing initiative, aligned to the Measures of Success framework.	Cabinet has established a data collection protocol, including individuals responsible. Data collection is underway and on-track.	Cabinet has routinized the review, discussion, and use of Measures of Success. Plans exist to support formative and summative evaluations of key strategies.	· · ·	· · ·

TABLE 5.2 Investment and sustainability rubric

INSTRUCTIONS: Highlight the stage that best represents your community. In the "Evidence" box, provide bullet-level evidence of that determination.

	Establishing . . .	. . . and Developing . . .	. . . and Mature	Evidence	Next Steps
Financial support	Cabinet has documented a budget and fundraising plan, with personnel dedicated to fundraising.	Some public and private funding has been secured, as well as strategic and in-kind support.	The work is fully funded for 3–5 years through diverse funding sources.	· · ·	· · ·
Execution infrastructure	A subset of individuals, perhaps from a small number of agencies or organizations, lead and execute the bulk of the work.	Working groups are clearly structured, functioning, and productive.	Established backbone organization with dedicated staff to support facilitation, data collection, and communication management.	· · ·	· · ·
Implementation strategy	Key initiatives are identified or underway.	There is a documented implementation plan with clearly identified activities, roles, and timelines, includes responsibilities for all participating Cabinet agencies and institutions.	Has established a structure to support collaboration to execute plan and report and discuss progress at the Cabinet level.	· · ·	· · ·

	Establishing . . .	. . . and Developing . . .	. . . and Mature	Evidence	Next Steps
Movement building	Cabinet has established a plan to communicate and mobilize stakeholders around its efforts.	Effectively and regularly communicates to the community in ways that mobilize action.	Community members are regularly and actively engaged in advancing the agenda.	· · ·	· · ·

Review the Process Rubrics Regularly

The metrics only have value if they drive the work of the Cabinet. Cabinets need to regularly—every three or four months—review their progress on the process rubrics for committed leadership and investment and sustainability and on the quantitative measures of opportunity and outcomes. While some data may only be collected once or twice a year, looking at the metrics more often keeps everyone focused on the goals and ensures data are reviewed promptly once they are available.

USE A "THROUGHLINE" TO LINK GOALS, ACTIONS, AND OUTCOMES

The complexity of cross-sector collaboration can make it difficult to keep track of how the different elements fit together. A key companion piece to the Measures of Success framework is the "Throughline," a tool that succinctly captures the relationship between goals, actions, and outcomes for specific collaborative interventions. The Throughline can be used in combination with the Measures of Success framework to track progress toward specific goals of the collaborative action, access to services, and impact on children. When used with rubrics for committed leadership and investment and sustainability, a Throughline gives the Cabinet the tools it will need to keep an eye on how its work is proceeding. It starts by identifying a Cabinet goal and moves to the strategies, collaborative actions, quantifiable increases in services and supports, and finally to changes in child-level outcomes, as shown in table 5.3. For example, Somerville has identified improving kindergarten readiness as a key goal. To accomplish this, the Cabinet has achieved an investment and sustainability goal by raising funds to expand access to high-quality preschool slots. A target metric for opportunity and access is the number of children in the city enrolled in preschool, and a child outcomes metric is the average score on Somerville's kindergarten readiness assessment.

Part of the value of the Throughline is its ability to capture a coherent narrative of the work the Cabinet is doing and what it will accomplish. It can be used as a communication tool both with the

TABLE 5.3 Collaborative action Throughline

INSTRUCTIONS: The Throughline connects goals, actions, and outcomes. Start with the goal you aim to achieve, then identify the initiatives.

GOALS	COLLABORATIVE ACTION		ACCESS AND PARTICIPATION	CHILD/YOUTH IMPACT
Goals	**Initiatives**	**Strategies and actions**	**Measures of access and participation**	**Student outcomes**
This is the high-level student outcome you seek to achieve or improve. A strong goal is clear about WHO is expected to make WHAT achievement/improvement in a specific time frame (WHEN).	An initiative includes any structured, planned approach to take a series of actions in pursuit of the goal.	Identify specific strategies and actions deployed under the initiative.	Strong measures of access and participation will clearly identify WHAT and WHO are being measured. Indicate with a Yes/No if data will be disaggregated into smaller student subgroups in the Subgroups box.	Strong measures of student outcomes will clearly identify WHAT and WHO are being measured. Indicate with a Yes/No if data will be disaggregated into smaller student subgroups in the Subgroups box.
Example: Improve student literacy of middle schoolers in three years.	Expand out-of-school time learning	Establish new partnerships with afterschool partners.	# of formalized partnerships Subgroups (Y/N)	Subgroups (Y/N)
		Expand number of summer school seats.	# of available summer school seats # of students enrolled Subgroups (Y/N)	% of students experiencing summer reading loss of >5% Subgroups (Y/N)
		Audit summer and afterschool opportunities.	Subgroups (Y/N)	Subgroups (Y/N)

Cabinet and with the public to build a shared understanding of the relationship between goals, actions, and outcomes. Another benefit is its ability to clarify which metrics are achievable in what time frame. Progress on measures of access and participation will occur before changes to child-level outcomes. The Throughline creates a clear and logical progression in which important conditions change for children—such as increased access to health services or high-quality early childhood or afterschool programs—that then lead to improvements in outcomes. As with the overall Measures of Success framework, responsibility for collecting data needs to be explicitly assigned, and the Cabinet should embed a regular process for reviewing progress on the Throughline.

ACHIEVE QUICK WINS TO HELP SUSTAIN MOMENTUM

While collaborative action initiatives may be primarily focused on achieving their long-term goals for children, they should also be attentive to identifying quick wins that can help galvanize public support by showing progress on shorter-term metrics. The key is to avoid having this be an either/or (short term versus long term) proposition. Children have needs that are already known to communities, and interventions should not halt because of a comprehensive planning process. Communities should identify quantifiable metrics that can be improved in a relatively short time frame and use these to sustain enthusiasm and support. Here are a few strategies for attaining quick wins without sidetracking other efforts.

Partner with an Organization That Has Data Validating Its Approach

Partnering with an organization that has an established data tracking system and evidence of impact is one way to achieve and show results relatively quickly. Two By All Means communities, Salem and Chattanooga–Hamilton County, chose to partner with City Connects, which has a decades-long history of identifying the individual needs and interests of each student and providing them with a customized set of supports. Not only has City Connects developed a clear process for assessing individual student needs, but it conducts a community scan of available services at the outset of the partnership, tracks implementation fidelity and, at the end of three years, reports on student outcome data. This data strategy provides a useful set of measures for communities at different stages of the partnership and also offers a clear timeline for moving from process outcomes to student population ones.

Other effective partnerships include those with afterschool and summer program providers. For example, Breakthrough Greater Boston is an established program with which Somerville has successfully partnered to provide a rich summer and afterschool experience for middle school students. Another out-of-school provider, BELLXcel, has worked extensively with Providence on summer programs. Both Breakthrough and BELLXcel have excellent data tracking systems. The substantial increases in the number of students participating in high-quality summer and afterschool programming—Somerville, for example, has tripled this number—is one example of a quick, tangible win that matters for kids and can be clearly communicated to the broader community as a benefit of the Cabinet's work.

Look to Process and Opportunity Indicators

Measures of access and opportunity provide strong indicators of progress before an intervention yields child and youth outcome data. In the City Connects model that both Salem and Chattanooga–Hamilton County are using, for example, measures of student academic achievement are only collected at the start of the third year of program implementation, but data on the numbers of services and supports provided are available midway through the first year. Other examples of access and opportunity indicators are the number of high-quality preschool spots and the number of students who receive health screenings and services. Movement in these areas can be considered a quick win.

Build on Efforts Already Underway in the Community

Cross-sector collaboration does not start in a vacuum, and communities often have many initiatives already underway at the start of the collaboration that would benefit from greater visibility and a cross-sector approach. Raising the profile of one or two initiatives, including them on the Throughline, and amplifying them with the resources of the Cabinet are effective ways to get a quick win as well as to honor the work that has been ongoing in the community prior to the initiation of the collaborative action initiative.

Use Pre- and Post-Test Measures

While most outcomes take years to see, some types of activities offer opportunities for quick impact. If an initiative involves a potentially high-impact intervention over a defined time period, testing students on academic skills or giving a survey on engagement or self-efficacy at the beginning and end of the program can show growth during the program. This works well with intensive summer or vacation week programs, for example.

TRACK TRENDS AND ANALYZE IMPACT

There are two ways to use data to show impact: by tracking trends over time, or by conducting experimental or quasi-experimental research. The easier and more common approach is the former. This involves identifying relevant metrics, collecting data, and reporting on it over time. The more closely the metric is related to the intervention, the more reasonable it is to expect to see improvement. Tracking data trends shows how children are doing on relevant measures, but it does not enable determination of the causal impact of the intervention. Without experimental research, it is not possible to tell whether data trends are the result of a specific intervention or other things that might be happening at the same time.

Design Initiatives with Evaluation in Mind

Ideally, Cabinets would include—and fund—plans for an evaluation of the impact of programmatic initiatives from the outset. Doing this during the design phase could impact decisions about how to roll out a program in a way that could make a research design stronger, for example.

Use IDs That Are Already Linked with Other Data Systems

It is surprisingly common for new programs either not to use IDs at all as part of the enrollment and data collection process, especially in their early stages, or to use IDs that are specific to that program. Given the wealth of information already contained in data systems, using official IDs assigned by the state or city will enable data analysis of demographic and other characteristics of participants.

SHARE DATA ACROSS SECTORS WHILE ENSURING DATA SECURITY

As agencies begin working together to create integrated systems for children, they often find a need to share data. Providers of afterschool programs, for example, are better able to offer appropriate support for students when they know something about students' academic backgrounds and strengths and whether they have special learning needs. Linking social service and academic data can help both sectors provide referrals and support services.

Two laws govern much of the data in question: the Family Educational Rights and Privacy Act (FERPA), which codifies the laws on student data privacy, and the Health Insurance Portability and Accountability Act (HIPAA), which covers the confidentiality of medical records. Until recently, these two laws were seen as insurmountable barriers to sharing data across agencies, leaving those who wanted to share data with few options. In recent years, though, agencies and programs have worked to create data sharing agreements with impacts from creating detailed analyses of spending on children across sectors and linking social service referral information with school data to streamline and speed up the provision of services. The keys to sharing individual student data are the permission of parents and guardians and clear, effective protocols determining who has access to the data and responsibility for keeping data secure.[3]

Build Data Sharing Agreements on a Foundation of Trust

Sharing data while protecting student confidentiality involves more than overcoming technical obstacles. As the program manager of the

Partnership for Resilience has noted, building trust with the community is the key to reaching data sharing agreements. Parents have legitimate concerns about private information becoming public and potentially being used against them or their children. The data in question could include information about domestic abuse, homelessness, mental health issues, or involvement with the justice system, for example. From an agency perspective, sharing financial data could raise concerns about implications for shifting priorities or resources.

Clarify the Need and Purpose for Sharing Data

Enthusiasm for data sharing can sometimes take on a momentum of its own without a clear connection to its value. For data sharing to be worthwhile, there needs to be a defined, actionable purpose. For example, sharing student data with afterschool providers has value if the afterschool programs will be able to act on the information by changing their programming to better meet students' needs. If they have no plans to change their practice, sharing the data has little value.

Define Who Will Have Access to What Data

A key and natural concern for parents is who will have access to their children's information. Plans for sharing data need to include thoughtful provisions to ensure student and family privacy. Schools already have identified staff, such as counselors, with the training and need to access a broad set of student data, while teachers generally only have access to more limited information. Louisville, for example, is introducing a new data platform into the Jefferson County Public Schools that will link social services data with student data. Only specific people within the schools, though, such as trained resource coordinators, will be able to access these data through a limited set of licenses.

Consider More Robust Individual Records

While caution is advised in the sharing of data, our ability to be effective as a field and to meet children's needs will depend, in the long run, on our capacity to see and understand each student as an individual and respond as individual educators, and as a system, to that student's particular needs. This kind of case management system is common in medicine but the exception to the rule in education. The medical model includes regular data gathering on health factors and outcomes that is assembled in a portfolio, a medical record, and widely shared with medical providers in the interest of better serving the patient. The concept of a running record on a child's development and education is overdue in our field. Transcripts are too strictly limited to academic data. To better serve students, educators need a deeper, more holistic look at what is happening in the lives of children inside and outside of school. At EdRedesign, we have been developing this idea through our work on individual success planning, which we describe in the final chapter.

BEING THOUGHTFUL ABOUT ACCOUNTABILITY

One of the most sensitive areas of Cabinet work involves the decisions to select particular program providers to supply different services and implement the Cabinet's chosen strategies. These decisions are sometimes simple and straightforward, while at other times they can be complicated, involving competition between provider agencies, scarce resources, and local politics. Equally sensitive are judgments that Cabinets must make about agency performance in fulfillment of their contracts with the Cabinet. Clear expectations and agreed-upon criteria must be established at the outset of such contracts. Procedures for gathering and sharing performance data must be clear from the outset. Data can be a helpful tool in rationalizing decisions on providers.

Cabinets should consider carefully whether they want to attach performance targets to any contract. In an established field with clear metrics, targets may be desirable. In areas where experience is limited and metrics are less well defined, Cabinets will need to be cautious about explicit performance targets. In any event, data gathering on the performance of Cabinet-sponsored programs is critically important for the efficiency, effectiveness, and reputation of the Cabinet. Great care must be taken in establishing these data and accountability conditions.

This era of ubiquitous data brings with it ways to better understand who has access to opportunities and who does not. Data can help shine a light on a clearer pathway to realize the goals of collaborative action on behalf of children. They are powerful tools for establishing, defining, and sustaining collaborative action initiatives. Data are, in essence, vehicles for capturing the narrative of the collaborative action effort: its ambitions, its new opportunities, and its progress toward reaching its goals.

Key Tasks for Measuring Progress

- Conduct a gap analysis
- Choose metrics that will sustain collaborative action
- Use a measurement framework that captures the scope of the undertaking
- Achieve quick wins to help sustain momentum
- Track trends and analyze impact
- Share data across sectors while ensuring data security
- Be thoughtful about accountability

CHAPTER 6

Ensure Sustainability

There are multiple challenges that threaten the long-term sustainability of collaborative action efforts. These include changes in leadership; lack of reliable, structural funding; fading attention and public will; and shifting priorities, along with their complexity and long time horizon. For leaders to maintain the momentum of a cross-sector collaboration over time, careful planning and an adaptive strategy are necessary.

One of the biggest challenges to sustainability is the uncertain tenure of key leaders. Mayors are, by definition, temporary, and subject to periodic elections. Some even face term limits. When mayors take the lead in forming Cabinets, as is desirable, they also expose the Cabinet to a vulnerability that the founding mayor is succeeded by a new mayor who does not want to continue an initiative that is identified with her predecessor. This lack of continuity is a common phenomenon in government and can be fatal to various incarnations of collaborative action. Likewise, this succession challenge and threat also occurs with superintendents, whose tenures are sometimes even less predictable than those of mayors. Cabinets must recognize these risks at the outset of their work and, from the beginning, plan for sustainability. In the words of Dr. Bryan Johnson, superintendent of the Hamilton County Schools and a member of the Chattanooga–Hamilton County Children's Cabinet, "Our whole goal in becoming a part of the By All Means network and establishing a Children's Cabinet was to really break down those silos and to ensure that as we work together, we are intentional and thoughtful and set up systems, processes, and structures that outlive each of our tenures in our individual positions."

In order to mitigate succession risk, mayors, superintendents, and other Cabinet leaders must create sustainability plans that build in safeguards to prevent the work from being washed out due to leadership turnover. These plans should include institutionalizing the Cabinet, creating durable backbone support, securing both short- and long-term funding, and ensuring the effort has broad traction within the community. This last point is particularly important: ultimately, the only way to keep this work going is if the public demands it. Cabinets have a limited amount of time after their inception to prove a value proposition to the public and to partner organizations. If the value of collaborative action for children is clearly established, then various constituencies will insist on the work being carried forward regardless of changes in leadership. In this chapter, we present strategies for improving the chances of keeping a cross-sector collaboration going in the face of leadership turnover and other challenges.

INSTITUTIONALIZE THE CABINET

The best way to ensure the Cabinet's persistence through changes of leadership is to institutionalize it via an executive order or an official act of the local legislative governing body such as the city council. Unlike many statewide Children's Cabinets, local Cabinets are often initially established informally, without any official authority. They should take the cue from statewide Cabinets and codify their existence. This establishes the Cabinet as an official part of city government and makes it less tied to a specific mayor.

A mandate for a local Cabinet can come from the executive or legislative branches. A mayor or a city council can formally establish the existence of a collaborative action body and should also specify its membership and mandate. Denver's mayor, for example, established his city's Children's Cabinet through executive order, specifying that it would consist primarily of all municipal agencies with responsibility for children. Importantly, staffing for the Denver Children's Cabinet is also institutionalized, through the municipal Office of Children's Affairs. Several full-time staff members provide data and programmatic support to the Cabinet. Whenever possible, provisions for staffing and budget should be included.

ESTABLISH A ROBUST BACKBONE ORGANIZATION

Cabinets need to create a robust backbone structure to hold and implement the full vision of the Cabinet while bringing new capacity and connective capability. The Cabinet members by themselves likely do not have the time to accomplish their goals. Cabinet members are generally executives who can develop a shared vision across sectors and make strategic and programmatic decisions involving their organizations, but they are not the ones who will carry out the actual work. Individual agencies can take on pieces of the implementation, but without the connective tissue of a backbone, the danger is that each agency will retreat into its own silo, negating the power of the Cabinet.

In the early days of a Cabinet, a single person may fill the backbone role, coordinating across agencies and ensuring that Cabinet members' designees carry out assigned tasks. It is important for this person to be seen as neutral and not representing the interests of just one of the entities on the Cabinet. Creating durable funding for this staff position ensures the function can be maintained over time. Some communities, such as Somerville, have one or two city or cross-agency staff members dedicated to supporting the Cabinet. To build greater capacity to carry out the work and raise funds, though, Cabinets should create a more formalized and robust backbone structure as soon as possible. Often, the backbone takes the form of an independent 501(c)(3) organization that can raise funds and implement key pieces of the cross-sector collaboration. The backbone can also carry out community engagement activities and public messaging campaigns.

In Tacoma, the Foundation for Tacoma Students serves as the backbone organization for the Graduate Tacoma collaborative. With a sizable staff of sixteen as well as a governing board, the foundation takes on a wide range of activities to fulfill its goal of "ensuring the continuity, stability and growth of the Graduate Tacoma community-wide movement." The foundation's responsibilities include extensive data collection and analysis, professional development, alignment of resources, and public advocacy and messaging. In Louisville, the nonprofit organization 55,000 Degrees initially served as the Cabinet's backbone organization. As the Cabinet structure and mission evolved under the new name Evolve502, Louisville created a new 501(c)(3) backbone organization. Through fundraising from local philanthropies, Evolve502 has hired an executive director and several other staff members to lead its Promise Scholarship effort as well as its other cross-sector work in support of children and youth. Other communities, though, have had more difficulty setting up their backbone organizations. Providence has filed paperwork establishing its backbone but has yet to hire staff or get it off the ground, and other cities have also struggled to fund support positions.

Lead backbone staff play an essential role in shaping and sustaining the Cabinet's work. Choosing staff wisely is critically important, as these staff come to be the day-to-day face of the Cabinet's work. In addition to various technical competencies, staff need well-developed interpersonal skills and the ability to navigate the political and logistical complexities that often determine the work's success. Effective backbone staffing involves understanding the interests and experiences of different constituencies, while envisioning the full potential of the Cabinet.

Key competencies for this role include:

- A high degree of comfort working with top-level leaders, including the mayor, superintendent, and other key municipal leaders
- Deep knowledge of the community, its history, its constituencies, and its most pressing issues
- The ability to gain the trust of multiple constituencies and to be seen as a neutral, honest broker who is not favoring one set of interests over another

- Skill in fundraising, both for the backbone itself and for the ongoing actions of the Cabinet
- The capacity to oversee multiple, complex projects; run meetings; develop action steps; and ensure they're carried out
- Well-developed interpersonal skills and cultural competency that enable the staffer to be a regular boundary crosser, communicating and working effectively with all kinds of people and groups in the community.

DISTRIBUTE LEADERSHIP AND FORM PARTNERSHIPS

Cabinets need to quickly find a balance between mayoral control and more broadly distributed leadership. To accomplish this, the multisector nature of the collaborative action effort is an important asset since it naturally lends itself to shared action and responsibility. The school superintendent and school board should be key allies from the start and should take a central role in identifying both needs and solutions. But other organizational partners, as well as staff throughout the different organizations, should also see their essential roles in the success of the collaboration. In Louisville, for example, the Metro United Way has taken the lead, in partnership with the Jefferson County Public Schools and the Unite Us platform, on defining the scope and function of a new data platform to improve youth referrals to services. In Illinois, the Partnership for Resilience works closely with Governors State University and a range of health-care providers to provide teacher training on trauma and direct services to students. This community-focused, distributed model extends the work into the community and, by adding value, creates an expectation that these supports will continue.

CREATE A SUSTAINABLE FUNDING STRATEGY

Cabinets should create a comprehensive, long-term financing strategy. Sustained funding is essential for carrying out all aspects of the Cabinet's work, from supporting the functions of the Cabinet and backbone to financing the specific initiatives that benefit children.

The survival of cross-sector initiatives depends on securing reliable funding, which is a particular challenge during the current era of federal disinvestment in the social safety net and an economic downturn that is now decimating state and local budgets.

The Cabinet should establish as a core value the need to prioritize funding for children. Everyone from the mayor to the superintendent to backbone staff and other Cabinet members should make the case publicly that changing life trajectories for vulnerable children requires a new community-wide social compact that includes, in the long term, a new commitment to public investment. The public needs to view the work of the Cabinet as central to the government's responsibility to its residents. Being specific about the tangible benefits of the Cabinet's work can help make this case, as can moral arguments about basic fairness, equal opportunity, and the life and learning conditions each child deserves. Leaders can marshal powerful equity arguments, based on data, to make the case for increased investment in children's well-being, especially for subgroups of children who have been marginalized due to race, class, disability, ethnicity, and language.

At the outset of the cross-sector collaboration, it may be possible to form a Cabinet and do some early work without additional funding by using existing staff who are loaned from Cabinet members' agencies. However, this is not a viable, long-term strategy. In the words of Children's Funding Project director Elizabeth Gaines, "What gets funded gets done." Cabinets need dedicated backbone support as well as money to support programmatic initiatives. Cabinets should make developing a funding strategy a top priority, while acknowledging that, in the near term at least, the community's ambitions are likely to be tempered by what is financially feasible. The Children's Funding Project, a nonprofit organization that tackles the thorny issue of funding comprehensive strategies for improving children's outcomes, advocates a multipronged "find, align, generate" strategy that includes finding new funding, aligning existing funds, and generating new revenue. Only the third, generating new revenue, ensures long-term stability. While it takes substantial effort, an increasing number of communities are achieving this goal.

Conduct a Fiscal Analysis

The first step Cabinets should take in developing a funding strategy is to examine current revenue and expenditures for education, after-school and summer programs, and other services and enrichment programs for children. It is important for Cabinet members to understand how the funding of each agency works—what percent comes from the federal and state governments, what are the main spending categories, and which financial pressures and constraints each organization feels. The siloed nature of the existing system means it is likely that few have a clear understanding of other sectors. The Children's Funding Project has developed a process for creating a detailed fiscal map, which many communities have chosen to use.

Calculate the Costs Associated with Different Components of the Work

Next, the Cabinet should calculate the anticipated costs for its own work and backbone support—including staffing, space, and materials—as well as for programmatic elements of its work. The costs associated with actual initiatives vary widely by type, scope, and community size. Cabinets must consider the long-term costs of a particular strategy and, before launching an initiative, develop a viable plan for meeting those costs. Cabinets should be realistic while at the same time, aspirational. Instituting universal preK, for example, is a goal of many communities, but one few are able to finance in the absence of state and federal funding. Increasing summer learning opportunities or the number of mental health counselors in schools may still be hard to fund, but upgrading these services is generally less costly than financing a new universal entitlement. Building a fully realized cradle-to-career pipeline complemented by systems of support and opportunity is too expensive for any community to address in the near term. Cabinets must set priorities, identifying component parts of an overall system that can be built out sequentially.

This analysis of programmatic options and possible funding sources should be a key element of the strategy selection process. As we discussed in chapter 4, considerations of funding and activities are iterative and deeply embedded in decisions about which actions to undertake: in Louisville, for example, the estimation of the full cost of providing Promise Scholarships to all students led to a substantial scaling back of that effort. Conversely, Somerville has been able to substantially expand its early childhood initiatives after receiving several large grants for their work. Cabinets need to be opportunistic, putting pieces in place that have specific, likely funding sources while working to secure more generalized, comprehensive funding.

Identify Potential Sources of Funding

Cabinets should include as wide a range of funding options as possible in their financial strategies within the Children's Funding Project's "find, align, generate" categories.

Find

To find new money, look to foundations or untapped government funding opportunities. Foundation funding can be essential for getting an initiative off the ground, and in some cases, it can even represent a long-term commitment to cross-sector work. Communities with robust local philanthropy are at an advantage in this, as many foundations exclusively fund work within specific geographic jurisdictions. Many foundations prefer to fund start-up work and new initiatives rather than to provide ongoing programmatic support, so this is often a short-term option. Less commonly, local foundations may be willing to make an intensive, extended commitment. Generally, Cabinets should avoid long-term reliance on philanthropy to sustain particular initiatives. Not only are philanthropies unlikely to supply such funding, but the services, supports, and opportunities that Cabinets envision for children should ultimately be a civic responsibility.

Graduate Tacoma's work, for example, originated and continues to be funded through a partnership of local foundations after more than a decade in operation. Other options for finding funding include community benefits agreements funds, payments in lieu of taxes, and government grants designed for specific purposes. In Oakland, Mayor Libby Schaaf has embraced the role of fundraiser-in-chief, spearheading a major, multiyear effort to create a foundation to support services for children and youth long into the future. As part of the Oakland Promise's cradle-to-career initiative, Schaaf has put her political capital and fundraising acumen into raising money that seeds college savings accounts, provides college scholarships, and funds other programs.

Align

Using the information from the fiscal analysis, Cabinets can identify opportunities to realign spending with priorities. A strength of the Cabinet is its function to improve both information and resource sharing across agencies and organizations. In Denver, for example, Mayor Michael Hancock has established a Children's Cabinet consisting of all city agencies with responsibility for children. An express purpose of the Cabinet is to align and coordinate funding for children and to ensure funds are targeted to areas of greatest priority. This also helps avoid either duplication or gaps in programming for children and youth. Efficiency of current spending is an important Cabinet concern.

Generate

The best way to ensure sustained financial support is to generate new, permanent funding streams. This generally means raising taxes in one form or another, which always comes with substantial political risks and the difficult task of persuasion. Cabinets can be potent advocates for policy and budgetary changes that affect the flow of resources to children. It is important, albeit challenging, for Cabinets to consider nonpartisan strategies of advocating for the resources needed for children's well-being. Community leaders are well positioned to make a clear and compelling case, at the local, state, and federal levels, for public investment in children. Such work, in itself, takes enhanced capacity, and that must be considered in setting Cabinet priorities.

Ultimately, the Cabinet is making the case for communities to assume a broader range of responsibilities for their children, a new social compact. The Children's Funding Project has worked successfully with numerous cities and counties such as Denver; San Antonio,

Texas; Portland, Oregon; and Broward County, Florida, to make the case for increased public funding.[1] In others, campaigns have not been successful, although sometimes a second attempt can be successful when the first is not.

JOIN A NETWORK

Joining a network that supports cross-sector collaboration provides critical support to communities and helps leaders and staff buffer the sense that this work can be overwhelming. A key finding for us, learned from our By All Means consortium over the past four years, is the benefit communities have derived from being part of a cohort-based network. By All Means provides tangible support through direct consultation, twice-yearly meetings, access to outside expertise, and assistance on topics ranging from community engagement to data. While these components have been important to communities, the less tangible elements have also been invaluable for the shared experience across communities working toward common broad goals.

By All Means is just one of several networks supporting cross-sector collaboration. A number of other integrated support organizations—notably, StriveTogether, Promise Neighborhoods, the Forum for Youth Investment, the Coalition for Community Schools and Communities in Schools—also use a network-of-communities approach. The Local Children's Cabinet Network, which is jointly organized by EdRedesign, the Children's Funding Project, and the Forum for Youth Investment, is another network with fairly open membership that supports local communities with Children's Cabinets.

Our research with By All Means communities revealed several key benefits of participating in a network of cross-sector collaborations.

Cross-Community Learning

Coming together for regular meetings strengthens each community's partnership, while also enabling cross-community learning. The meetings are a way to share information across communities and build, over time, trusted relationships that facilitate cross-community sharing of effective practices and problem solving. Initially, the in-person nature of meetings creates an important forum for building relationships through informal conversations between sessions and during social times. As our network has matured, members have become increasingly likely to connect outside of the meetings to learn from and support each other.

Leadership Support

Acknowledging the unique leadership challenges of cross-sector collaboration, the By All Means consortium has included exclusive sessions to support mayors and superintendents. These key leaders have formed their own cohort of support, with opportunities to share openly the challenges, concerns, and successes of the efforts in their communities. As with the broader set of community representatives, these relationships have strengthened over time and have enabled these leaders to turn to each other at moments of crisis and for inspiration.

Strengthened Community Teams

A surprising finding from our By All Means consortium is the value that community teams find in meeting intensively off-site. Whether team members are coming from a few miles or a few thousand miles away, they find that being away from their communities gives them a clearer focus with fewer distractions and is an opportunity to dive into their work more intensively than they can do at home. Over time, By All Means has increased the amount of time dedicated to community team meetings during the twice-yearly convenings.

- *Outside expertise.* The network serves as a backbone support to each individual Cabinet and backbone, providing a framework and broad direction, lessons from others who are further in the process, and expertise in specific areas. While the meetings are one way of bringing together resources on everything from community engagement to early childhood development to the social determinants of health to funding, direct support from various experts—including those within each member community—can offer more targeted technical assistance to individual communities as well.
- *Legitimacy and political support.* Being part of a network also brings the added legitimacy of a broader, widely recognized move-

ment, which can be particularly helpful in showing that cross-sector strategies are being embraced by communities nationwide.

- *External accountability.* Sharing updates on progress during regular cross-community calls and, more publicly, at national meetings brings a degree of external accountability to cross-sector collaboration. There's a positive peer-pressure effect, with communities wanting to show they are accomplishing important goals. Some networks also bring external accountability through the public reporting of outcome and opportunity metrics.

DEVELOP A PUBLIC COMMUNICATIONS STRATEGY

Cabinets should develop and implement a communications strategy to galvanize the public in support of an ambitious vision for new systems of opportunity and support. Branding the effort helps raise its profile and create a common message about the effort. Somerville has named its collaborative youth effort SomerPromise. The two collaborations in Illinois are called the Partnership for Resilience and Resilient Southern Illinois, emphasizing their focus on youth trauma. Tacoma's name reflects its primary goal: Graduate Tacoma.

Sharing progress on key metrics should be a key part of the communications strategy. We discuss in an earlier chapter the importance of metrics for telling the story of the collaborative effort, and it is important to highlight tangible progress as part of the broader communication strategy. These metrics should resonate with the community as meaningful indicators of progress, but they do not necessarily need to focus on child outcomes initially. For example, raising a substantial amount of money for specific initiatives is one way to show progress; increasing the number of students receiving services or participating in programming is another.

PLAN FOR CABINET TURNOVER

Turnover among Cabinet members is inevitable. Anticipating this turnover can go a long way toward mitigating its impact. The loss of key participants—especially those who have central roles in the work—is always disruptive, but it does not need to derail the ongoing work. Sharing decision-making on the Cabinet is one way to insulate the work against change. If each member of the Cabinet has had a voice and feels invested in the Cabinet's strategies and actions, the loss of a single member won't have as big an effect as it would if just one or two members were doing the bulk of the work and simply telling the others about it during meetings.

Another effective strategy for ensuring the continuity of the work is to create a journey map that documents the key decisions and actions of the Cabinet. Even Cabinets without major turnover have found the maps helpful, but they are particularly valuable for quickly orienting new Cabinet members, as well as new backbone staff, to the work. A journey map, such as the example created by the Chattanooga–Hamilton County Children's Cabinet in figure 6.1, can be simple or more complex, but it should capture some of the rationale for the choices the Cabinet has made as well as a timeline of actions.

Finally, local champions, civic leaders from the private and public sectors, current or former CEOs, congressmen and -women, former mayors, community-based organization leaders, and others can be valuable assets in advocating for the continuity of Cabinet work. Especially when Cabinets are led by elected officials, it is important to have other community leaders, whether formally or informally, associated with and advocating for the work of the Cabinet. In southern Illinois, for example, Glenn Poshard is an ideal champion for the Partnership for Resilience. He previously served as a US representative, president of the University of Southern Illinois, and a state senator, and he currently heads one of the region's philanthropies. As a well-known, trusted, homegrown leader who has influence and commands respect in the community and beyond, his support and influence on behalf of the partnership are invaluable.

There are numerous challenges to sustaining cross-sector collaboration, but successful Cabinets recognize this from the outset and build in safeguards to insulate their initiatives from changes in leadership, funding, and other challenges. Partnering with the community in envisioning and implementing a new system of child support and education, securing long-term funding, and institutionalizing the work to protect against turnover can all help ensure the long-term continuity of the effort.

FIGURE 6.1 Hamilton County's journey map

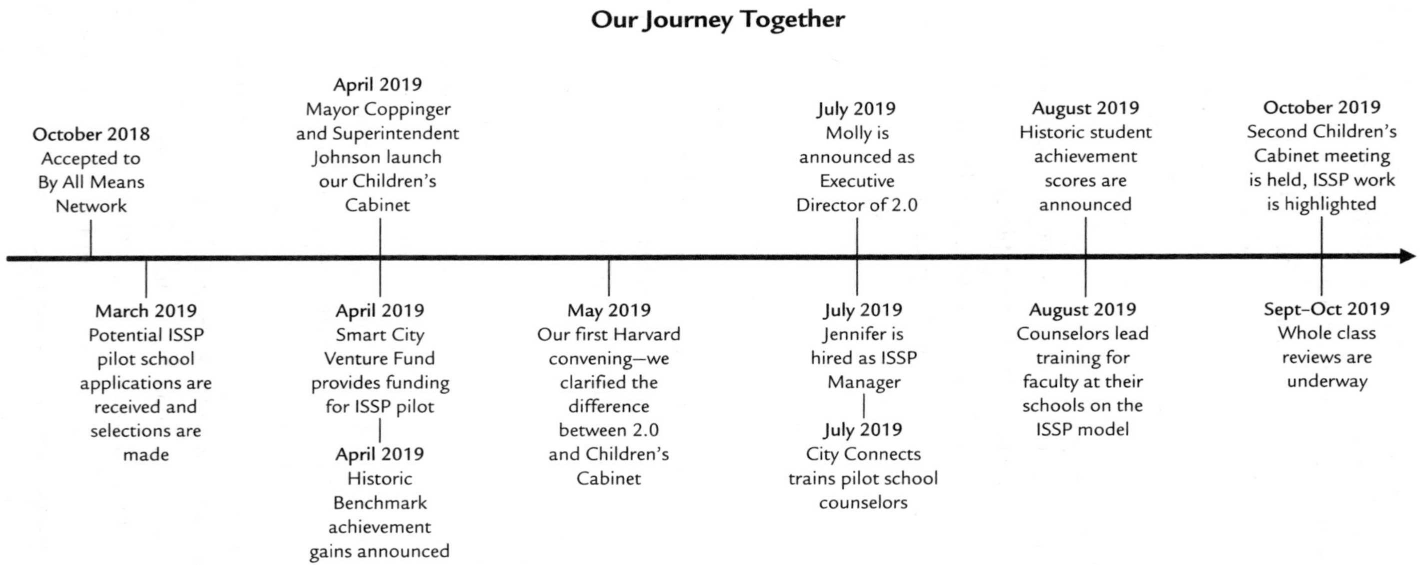

Key Tasks for Ensuring Sustainability

- Institutionalize the Cabinet
- Establish a robust backbone organization
- Distribute leadership and form partnerships
- Create a sustainable funding strategy
- Join a network
- Develop a public communications strategy
- Plan for Cabinet turnover

CHAPTER 7

Envisioning and Creating a Better, Fairer Future

Our world has altered since we commenced the journey of writing this book. The Covid-19 pandemic and the sweeping movement for racial justice have not only brought short-term disruptions to daily life and the status quo, but set in motion long-term changes in our society and culture. It is too early to tell how and how much our policies and practices will change, whether in the field of education, child development, health care, or policing, but there is no doubt at all that America's profound experiences of 2020 will leave an indelible mark on this country. Talk of change is in the air everywhere. Yet at the same time, people have been traumatized and are recovering from the loss, anger, frustration, and anxiety brought about by Covid-19 and the murders of George Floyd and other Black men and women. Some changes need to be immediate and are already happening, literally overnight. Others will take more time. Children's Cabinets are ideal venues and catalysts for discussing, conceiving, and implementing these changes.

These crises have exposed to the general public the profound inequities that are the lived experience of those victimized by marginalization, racism, and economic insecurity in our society. As Paul Reville (one of the authors) recently argued in the *Boston Globe*, "The widespread, long-term closing of schools has now revealed to the nation the gross inequities that have always existed in the lives of impoverished families and children. Suddenly, we see front page stories and lead editorials on topics like uneven Internet and technology access, food insecurity, and limited access to physical and mental health services. It's as though a tidal wave has pulled back the ocean to reveal the ocean floor and the uncomfortable realities of life beneath the surface."[1] The general public's awareness and sense of urgency about inequity has increased, and Children's Cabinets are well positioned to seize this moment and guide action for change. The work of collaborative action, Children's Cabinets, and building cradle-to-career systems of education, support, and opportunity is more urgent now than ever before. The movement is growing and is poised to assume leadership in responding to the near- and long-term needs of our children, families, and communities.

This book has focused on how to do the work of collaborative action in response to the compelling need for transformed, equitable systems of child development and education to serve the nation's children. Children's Cabinets are the vehicles for reconceptualizing the systems, building public support, and planning and executing implementation of more robust services, supports, and learning opportunities for children and youth. In this historic moment of change, Cabinets have the opportunity to lead the conversation aimed at creating a new social compact and building new structures and systems of education, support, and opportunity for children. Cabinets are also well positioned to show their value immediately by responding to the current crisis of school closing and social unrest. In many communities, the Cabinets have proved ideal venues for the coordination of supports and services ranging from food to Wi-Fi. Cabinets are also places where leaders from throughout the community can come together to discuss tough, sensitive subjects like racial justice and police brutality.

CHILDREN'S CABINETS ADAPT TO NEW CHALLENGES

We have observed that under the pressure of these crises, communities have been turning to Children's Cabinets as places to shape communications strategies, coordinate the delivery of vital services, gather data on needs and gaps in support, and host difficult conversations on sensitive issues that threaten to divide communities. Chattanooga–Hamilton County, for example, has been using its Children's Cabinet as a de facto situation room for coordinating its child- and family-focused response to the pandemic. The Cabinet began meeting weekly in March 2020 to ensure a unified, cross-sector approach to the crisis. According to Hamilton County Public Schools superintendent Dr. Bryan Johnson, "When we look at the Children's Cabinet, the systems and structures were already set up, and it speaks volumes for how quickly and effectively we've been able to respond as a community." In Louisville, the backbone organization Evolve502 has similarly been convening a working group of the Cabinet to coordinate services for children during the pandemic. Jefferson County Public Schools director of policy and systems Jonathan Lowe says the urgency and focus of the Covid-19 response effort has, in fact, made the value of the Cabinet more apparent and given it a clearer shared purpose.

As these examples suggest, Children's Cabinets are evolving to meet pressing community needs. We expect this evolution to continue and accelerate as these Cabinets prove their value, demonstrate their capacity, engage more and more people, and make a difference in their communities. As this happens, community investment in the work of the Cabinet and its associated backbone organization will increase, thus elevating the public perception of the Cabinet and opening the way for it to become a central, driving force for short- and long-term change.

Cabinets have the potential to engineer monumental, paradigmatic shifts in the way communities view and exercise their responsibilities for rearing, developing, and educating their children. With their underlying values sharply focused on equity, Cabinets can lead a social justice movement, one that uses this moment to build a better system for all. To do so will require communities to step back and consider the shortcomings and unfairness embedded in their current systems, while at the same time envisioning what needs to change and how to change it. This thinking must be expansive, imaginative, and challenging to the legacy system.

This process should be intentional, reflective, and inclusive. It should be an exercise in strategic thinking, but one that is creative and out of the box, pushing the parameters and confines of the status quo.

ENVISIONING PARADIGM SHIFTS

Cabinets Pitch the Community

In bringing people to the planning table, Cabinet leaders must present a compelling value proposition to various community members and leaders. It goes something like this:

Large-scale disruption, such as we've suffered in recent months, presents both danger and opportunity. The dangers are obvious, life-and-death threats including economic catastrophe, job loss, housing instability and homelessness, lack of access to quality health care, and personal safety threats. At the same time, dramatically raised public consciousness on matters of equity and social justice do present opportunities for change, ranging from minor technical and symbolic tinkering to major paradigm shifts.

The education sector, for example, has been traumatized by the school closings. It needs to recover its equilibrium before becoming open to embracing life-changing paradigm shifts. Nonetheless, now is the time for urgent, thoughtful contemplation of the ways in which this moment can be turned into a movement for major transformation. This is the time to call together all voices to envision changes that will, for example, eradicate childhood poverty, attack racism in all its forms, and improve the quality of our systems of child development and education to dramatically increase the well-being and educational achievement and attainment of those who our education has least well served. This is a time for the radical reinvention of what happens inside of schools, our approaches to curriculum and instruction at all levels of our education system. It is also the time for demanding that society put in place the basic supports—food, housing, health care, and safety—that children need in order to be ready to learn. We must now remedy profound opportunity gaps, notably making sure that all children have access to quality enrichment opportunities in the 80 percent of their waking hours they spend outside of school. The window for progress on changes of this scope will not be open forever, and those who seek to take advantage of this moment for substantial system change must be prepared.

Children's Cabinets should consider the following seven major shifts as they set and revisit goals for collaborative action in the future.

BUILDING CRADLE-TO-CAREER SUPPORT SYSTEMS TO ENABLE LIFELONG LEARNING

If we are to prepare all of our children to fulfill their promise and be successful in work, citizenship, and family life, then we need to attack poverty and its insidious effects on families and children. Many other nations have long ago concluded that there is both a moral obligation and an economic imperative to have systems of universal health care, early childhood education, paid family leave, housing stability, and access to nutritious food as minimum requirements for family stability and children's well-being. Without addressing these challenges, it will be virtually impossible for schools as we know them, no matter how significantly reformed, to be successful in doing what our leaders have appropriately asked schools to do: educate every child to high levels.

Given the rapidly and continuously changing requirements of twenty-first-century work and democracy, nations will have to cultivate human talent as never before. To be successful in the twenty-first century requires continuous learning through all stages of life. Continuous learning from the earliest stages of life to mature adulthood should be the norm if our citizens and society are to adapt to the changing economic environment and prosper in coming decades. Individual citizens and the entire society have a shared interest in lifelong learning. For individuals, the benefits are obvious, starting with "the more you learn, the more you earn." There are clear ethical reasons to commit to giving every child a fair chance to realize their full potential, but we also have economic imperatives that necessitate educating our population to the maximum degree so that our nation can prosper and remain competitive in a twenty-first-century, high-skill, high-knowledge economy. We desperately need a highly educated, media-literate citizenry capable of discerning truth, recognizing evidence, and engaging in sophisticated analytical thinking. We need a much higher percentage of our citizenry to be motivated and prepared to actively participate in the civic life of our challenging democracy. In coming years, human capital will be more important than ever to the prosperity of both our democracy and our economy. America has a long way to go in building a robust, nimble human capital development system to help our young people reach their full potential. Now is the time to redesign and rebuild.

Our current, somewhat sentimental ideas about schooling have severely constrained our conception of education. Now, we must move from an old-fashioned, schoolhouse-bound model of child development and education to a system of robust, flexible learning opportunities coupled with basic supports available from birth through adulthood. We need to break down the barriers of time and space that lock us into the narrow confines of schools by preparing for an education system that provides learning opportunities literally anytime, anywhere. We now have the technological tools and internet availability to do this, even if in the education sector, we haven't yet learned to use those tools very effectively. As we develop the education technology facility and capacity, we can begin to consider how we alter the structure and strategies of in-person education to maximize the value of critical learning relationships by creating structural and incentive changes to deepen and extend learning opportunities. Schooling conducted in person, at least in part, will always be with us, but it needn't be the entirety of what we consider education.

A place to start building a new conception of education is in our utilization of time. We could begin by acting on the strong research evidence showing that access to summer learning matters: those who get it surge forward, those who don't fall back and suffer learning loss. Access to summer learning is generally controlled by family wealth and social capital. Instead, we should be designing a system in which summer learning and enrichment are available to every child, not just to those fortunate enough to receive access through the accident of birth and family wealth. The same applies to learning opportunities after school and on weekends and holidays. It's time to bury our agrarian school calendar and substitute flexible, year-round learning (see Chiefs for Change and the Texas Education Agency for recent proposals on this topic). It's time to have a school schedule that reflects the realities of American family life in the twenty-first century. A nineteenth-century approach to the use of school time won't do it. Schedule changes are a prerequisite but not a substitute for major shifts in curriculum and instruction to deepen and broaden access to high-quality, engaging learning opportunities. To do all of this, we'll need to contemplate changes in teacher roles and schedules, adding new educational personnel, utilizing part-timers and community members, and national youth service corps members, while modularizing various elements of the curriculum and other learning opportunities.

Overall, we need to reconceptualize education as a lifelong function and build integrated systems so that early in their lives, children have access to high-quality teaching, content, enrichment opportunities, support, and the services necessary to propel them successfully through each stage of their development from birth to the acquisition of a quality job and then onward to give them the adaptive knowledge and tools they need to prosper in a constantly changing economy and democracy.

To create an effective governance mechanism for such a transformed system, we'll need to move beyond school boards to shape and govern a lifelong learning system. Our current governance structures are too fragmented, as we have observed in the helter-skelter, but well-intentioned response of the nation's school districts trying to figure out how to respond to the coronavirus. In the K–12 sector alone, we have more than 13,500 separate school districts, in addition to thousands of separately chartered and often separately governed charter schools. We have policy making at the federal, state, and local levels going on simultaneously and often moving in different directions. Our governance system is a recipe for incoherence.

Having separate boards for early childhood, K–12, and higher education, to say nothing of health and employment, means that our overall human development system (education and social services) is siloed, not integrated or comprehensive, not user-friendly or readily accessible to youth and families. Another problem is that these governance subsystems are frequently so heavily influenced by various constituencies that children's interests take a back seat. Our governance systems need to be more representative, broader in scope, and more seriously engaged in matters of policy, accountability, and connecting with the community. There is substantial resistance to any proposal for governance changes in these sectors, but advocates need to look for opportunities for achieving greater coherence.

Many powerful organizations across the country have worked on designs to advance some version or various aspects of the lifelong, holistic, integrated supports vision described above. A few examples are StriveTogether, Communities in Schools, the Coalition for Community Schools, Children's Aid Society, Harlem Children's Zone, Say Yes to Education, the Forum for Youth Investment, the Social Genome Project, and the Promise Neighborhoods Institute at PolicyLink. These, and many others, are pointing the way to the theory, practice, and evaluation of a "broader, bolder" conception of what needs to be done to guarantee that every childhood has sufficient education, support, and opportunity—in short, every child has ready access to a real pathway to success.

PROFESSIONALIZE FULL-ACCESS, HIGH-QUALITY, EARLY CHILDHOOD EDUCATION

Lifelong learning, as a right, should begin at birth. For years, brain science has shown that early childhood experiences significantly impact longer-term health, educational, and economic outcomes. The evidence is still incontrovertible: the most highly leveraged investments in education come in early childhood when children's brains are growing, developing, and vulnerable. Yet, the early childhood sector is the least adequately funded, least accessible, and least professionalized component of our education system. The pressures of the pandemic are causing the scaling back and closing of childcare facilities, further handicapping an already fragile sector. The growing gaps in access and quality are well known but seldom addressed. Early education teachers and personnel are woefully underpaid, and consequently, staff turnover in this field is unacceptably high, while attracting talent to the field is extremely challenging. States struggle to promote quality improvement systems, yet the lack of staffing continuity and general underfunding of the sector makes it difficult to enact high standards of quality.

Chronic, gross underfunding of this sector is the central problem. To wit, the most influential paradigm shift in this sector would be to raise teacher salaries and place them on a par with those of K–12 teachers. However costly, salary parity would bring about a sea change in the field. Secondly, early childhood, because of the shaky state of its finances, is too often thought of as important for three- to five-year-olds, but as a luxury from ages zero to three. While 80 percent of childhood brain growth occurs before age three and approximately half of children living in poverty in the United States begin school unequipped with foundational knowledge and skills, we do not have policies and supports to create anything approximating full access to the necessary supports and development interventions in the earliest years.

These are also the years in which children's brains are highly susceptible to trauma. We know that the fewer adversities a child experiences, the more likely they are to develop into a healthy adult. Much more protection and prevention work needs to be done with this age group, not only for the children, but also for and with families of our youngest people. Trauma-sensitive schools and other related organizations will be essential in the recovery from this Covid-19 crisis. Organizations like Turnaround for Children have provided strong leadership in the theory, science, and practice of trauma-sensitive practices and learning environments.

To advance this field overall, greater federal, state, and local funding accompanied by equitable, visionary policies will be essential. Philanthropic investments to conceptualize, trigger, and pilot change are necessary also, but should not be relied upon for permanent support of functions like education and child welfare, which are public responsibilities. Community organizations, like Children's Cabinets, can provide leadership, a forum for discussion and resolving differences, coordination, and advocacy for the appropriate policies and investments. Finally, early childhood education is an area in which the business community has been a powerful ally and champion for increased attention and funding. Its continued support is imperative.

INTEGRATED, PERSONALIZED EDUCATION AND SUPPORT

Perhaps the biggest shift of all would be to discard our factory system, one-size-fits-all, mass-production approach to education, replacing it with one that meets each child where they are and gives them what they need to be successful inside and outside of school. Such a personalized, customized approach begins with each child being seen and understood by adults within the education system, with families and educators coming together to decide what that child needs both inside and outside of school in order to thrive, achieve well-being, and be successful. This approach would require major restructuring of the existing systems, moving to a case management model, more like a medical system. It requires a mindset that distinguishes equity from equality and focuses on equity, a fair system that is responsive to each child. Equality is giving every child the same, while equity is giving each child what they need to achieve success. This kind of customized system requires great cultural sensitivity, given the diversity of our country. This will be a major reach for the education system but is a prerequisite for educating each child to his or her full potential.

Among the implications for schooling are significant changes to schedules, both the daily schedule and the yearly calendar. If we are to give each child the quality and quantity of instruction they need to achieve ambitious learning goals, then our rigid schedules will have to open up to accommodate the learning differences and variable needs among our students. This will be highly inconvenient for adults but essential to achieving the goal of meeting children where they are, as individuals, and giving them what they need to be successful in school and in life.

A personalized system is not exclusively or even primarily focused on academics, but also takes into account social and emotional learning and children's widely varying circumstances outside of school. Such considerations, in themselves, are a major shift for our education systems; however, this is not work for schools alone, because schools generally do not have the scope or capacity to solve pressing out-of-school challenges that impede student learning. In consequence, schools, operating on their own with a predominantly academic mission, have definitively proven not to have the capacity to equalize opportunity for young people in the United States. Mountains of data attest to this, not least of which are the data that persistently show the correlation between children's socioeconomic status and their educational achievement and attainment. Our only hope of breaking this iron law correlation is an individualized strategy that customizes education, opportunity, and support to meet the unique needs of each child.

A paradigm shift to personalization, to individual success planning for each child, will require a community-wide, comprehensive system beginning with integrated student supports, that is, coordination between the education system and a wide array of child- and youth-centered partners who deeply and regularly collaborate to meet young peoples' needs.

Integrated student supports (ISS), a concept that has been in use for decades, was further described in a book entitled *Broader, Bolder, Better: How Schools and Communities Help Students Overcome the Disadvantages of Poverty*, which Elaine Weiss and Paul Reville published in 2019.[2] They describe how various communities are coming together to offer children the kinds of supports and opportunities that are always available to children born into privilege, but often denied to disadvantaged children. ISS envisions a system in which every child receives the nurturance, health care, support, and stability they need to come to school every day ready to learn. Further, ISS pushes to provide students the kind of out-of-school learning opportunities in summer and after school that are not equitably available. The basic theory of action is that until we do for all children, in the way of opportunity and support, what those of us who have privilege do for our own, then there is no hope of schools, by themselves, preparing all children for success.

Personalized success plans as proposed by Harvard's Education Redesign Lab, which are tailored to each and every young person, are an especially promising strategy, and there is a growing body of research about their impact. These personalized plans are tools as well as processes for capturing the full range of strengths and needs of children and youth in order to connect them with tailored, seamless, and equitable services and opportunities. Conceptually, the plans represent our commitment to meet all children and youth where they are and give them what they need, inside of school and out, to be successful. Practically, success plans are logical tools with which to build new systems focused on *individual* needs. Leading the success planning process is a personal navigator, an educator who takes responsibility for overseeing the educational progress of the student; meeting with their family; shaping, implementing, and evaluating plans; and persistently following that child through multiple years of schooling. Building relationships and attacking the problem of student anonymity in our schools through the use of navigators would be a major step toward personalizing education and customizing our approach to each unique student.

The development of a system of navigators and success plans for each student is a major undertaking with serious implications for staffing, data gathering, and privacy, to name just several of the biggest challenges, but the potential benefits to students, teachers, and families are enormous. Strategically, the adoption of a student success planning approach signals the end of the factory model of education and the start of an era in which each child is seen and matters.

EQUITABLE, ONLINE LEARNING

The school closings precipitated by the pandemic have catapulted a reluctant education sector into the twenty-first-century world of educational technology. We've always been laggards when compared to the business sector or medicine. Now, it's time to catch up. With the increasing reliance on technology to fill the gaps created when schools partially or fully close, we've now been forced to witness the "digital divide," the unequal access to educational technology and services. Educators and our school systems now have a digital imperative to recognize and capitalize on the power and potential of online learning. Many of our school systems are still in the early stages of what can only be characterized as emergency adaptations to the sudden crisis of school closings. Education leaders are now struggling to identify the best tools and practices to bring state-of-the-art online learning opportunities to all of their students. They will need help—financing, expertise, and time for training and implementation—in order to succeed in this long overdue transformation. To be clear, schools will need to get everyone the equipment they need to participate online. Then every student's home will need Wi-Fi/internet access. Districts will need to make informed decisions about platforms, applications, and curricula to be delivered online. Teachers will need training and the time for it, and families will need technical support to get online access and consistent educational guidance in how to best support their learners. Finally, schools will need tutors, curators, and other new educational role players to support the operation of a 24/7, 365-day learning system. This is a heavy lift and will not be fully accomplished in the immediate future, but necessity has dictated progress, and the field is already making headway.

It's impossible to overstate the impact of the sudden but profound shift to online learning brought about by Covid-19. The genie is now out of the bottle in the world of education, and it's a safe prediction that things will never be the same. The advent of online learning will open up a vast array of opportunities, while at the same time presenting school systems, teachers, families, and students with an overwhelming number of choices about technical and substantive education matters—choices many will not have the capacity, information, expertise, and experience to make. National organizations, federal and state governments, and entrepreneurs of all kinds can be helpful in curating the choices and supplying evidence to help key players make informed decisions. District leaders are going to have to commit to a substantial investment in professional development to help teachers, many of whom have highly limited experience in this area, to adapt to and ultimately embrace new tools and modalities.

The embrace of contemporary educational technology must be guided, as initial efforts during the Covid-19 crisis have been, by relentless attention to all the dimensions of equity raised by greater reliance on technology. There is a real and present danger that the rushed embrace of education technology will create even more significant opportunity and achievement gaps. All the dimensions of tech adoption, from equipment to internet access, training and support, parental capacities and access, and technical assistance, have the potential to either close or widen the digital divide. Great care must be taken to close that divide and use these new tools to create a better, fairer distribution of learning opportunities.

A sequenced embrace of educational technology is a multiyear process and requires thoughtful staging. Demands will be high in the near term for school systems to shift from the emergency tech adaptations made during a precipitous crisis to a more intentional embrace of best practices and the development of a permanent, integrated system of educational technology. These changes won't happen overnight, but, in time, they will have a profound effect on learning possibilities and access to opportunity for children all across the country.

Not only will technology change the delivery of education, but the content will change (see the section on "Deeper Learning"), while new challenges such as nurturing the relationships at the heart of education will be front and center. Thought leaders in this domain of linking digital delivery with innovative content include Summit Learning, School of One, the Christensen Institute, the Florida Virtual School, and Next Generation Learning.

DESIGN FOR NURTURING RELATIONSHIPS

The biggest casualty of school closings has been relationships between students and their peers and their educators. Top priority must be given when schools reopen, whether in person or online, to designing our education systems to prioritize high-quality interpersonal relationships. Education, as defined in the Mandarin language, is about both teaching and nurturance. Our current education system is populated by teachers who care deeply about nurturance, but generally the structures and incentives of the system ignore the necessity of relationships in the process of learning. A paradigm shift in this area will require new roles for teachers and staff; new, more flexible personnel; changes in accountability measures to prioritize students' well-being; and connectedness as well as changes in structure, particularly in middle and secondary schools, where current structures often mitigate against quality relationship formation. No student should go through a school year anonymously. Practices like guidance-counselor-to-student ratios of 1:400, teachers seeing 150 students a week, and students juggling six or seven classes at a time must be reconsidered and replaced.

Each child needs an educator advocate, a navigator, who follows and cares for that child for the duration of their experience in a particular school. Secondary school homerooms should all be converted to "advisories," periods of time when teachers and students interact for a few hours each week on respective journeys through the education system, their challenges, families, hopes, and needs as they navigate the turbulent waters of adolescence in a changing society. Teachers crave deeper relationships with their students, and tools like success plans provide processes for permanently building those relationships.

Extracurricular activities are critical also. They are often the chief motivators drawing young people to school, and they should be prioritized, rather than cut the moment budget pressure increases. These activities, from sports to music to community service, are powerful means for building student confidence and motivation. They are also ideal venues for developing high-quality, working relationships between students, their peers, and the adults in their communities. Through intensive, extended engagement, students will draw strength and resilience from their relationships with peers and educators.

This emphasis on nurturing high-quality educational relationships, especially mentoring and advocacy for each individual student, is not just a response to this crisis but a necessary, permanent reform to our education system. This need will also increase in direct proportion to our utilization of remote learning tools and processes.

FAMILY ENGAGEMENT

For too long, the education system has, with some notable exceptions, given lip service to the importance of family engagement. In reality, most schools, most of the time, have regarded family engagement as a "nice to do" secondary or tertiary task. In the worst cases, schools sometimes have ignored family engagement altogether, trivialized it by overfocusing on parents' attendance at meetings, or simply regarded family involvement as a nuisance. Suddenly, the Covid-19 crisis has irretrievably thrust families into the very center of the education equation. While educators have long recognized that families are the first and long-term teachers of the children, too little has been done to enlist the partnership of parents in the educational mission of the schools. With all children learning at home for the fourth quarter of the 2019–2020 academic year and most for substantial portions of the 2020–2021 academic year, we've learned that if a one-size-fits-all approach doesn't work very well for students, it works even less well for families because of the wide variability in family circumstances, home environments, parent or guardian availability due to job requirements, language barriers, technology familiarity, and general education background.

There is an urgent need now to establish mechanisms of communication, relationship building, guidance, support, and technical assistance—all targeted toward helping parents to be effective supporters and nurturers of student learning. Family empowerment needs to be a top priority for leaders, school accountability systems, and educator training. Many challenges of language and culture exist in this field, and cross-cultural competency for educators will be of paramount importance and should be an essential part of preservice and in-service training. Again, in this area, we are blessed by examples of many schools that already have fully engaged parent partnership programs. There are also outstanding examples of individuals and organizations from the National PTA, to Harvard professor Karen Mapp and her Dual Capacity-Building Framework, to 1647: Connecting Families & Schools, the KIPP Schools, and many more that have long track records in trying to build effective school-family partnerships. Now is the time for a breakthrough in this area, for genuine, communicative, collaborative partnerships between educators and parents.

The kinds of changes we are proposing here are generational in nature, just as the opportunities and interventions designed to achieve equity and excellence in education must be extended over generations. Those working on family-centered, multigenerational support and development are leading the way in a broader concept, beyond a simply school-based strategy, for ensuring the health and well-being of students by recognizing and acting on the idea that in order for the child to flourish, the family must be healthy and stable. Interventions targeted at parents and guardians are critical. The multigenerational work of the Northside Achievement Zone (Minneapolis) and EMPath is exemplary in this field.

DEEPER LEARNING

The core of the education portion of child development is and should continue to be teaching and learning. However, our current models of curriculum and instruction have proved, well before the current crisis, not to be effective with significant proportions of our students. The advent of large-scale online learning has only compounded the need for radically redesigned approaches to curriculum and instruction. There is no shortage of theory, research, and best-practice examples to inform this shift, but a shift must happen. Students need to be engaged, connected, and experience rigor and relevance in their schoolwork. For too many children, that's not happening.

It's time to enhance student agency in learning, to individually customize curriculum and instruction, to focus on real-world applications of knowledge and skill, employing projects, simulations, and utilizing students' local environments. As mentioned above, it's imperative to be intentional about creating environments and incentives for building meaningful, ongoing student-teacher relationships and positive group and team-building dynamics among students. All the while, education needs to be substantially increasing the emphasis on the interpersonal and social emotional skills that employers are now demanding. Organizations and models to lead the way in this kind of work are virtually unlimited: Jal Mehta's work on "deeper learning," Jobs for the Future's initiatives on career pathways, Year Up, the Campaign for Grade-Level Reading, the Collaborative for Academic, Social, and Emotional Learning (CASEL)'s framework on social and emotional learning, Big Picture's experience in community-based and project-based applied learning, High Tech High, mastery learning, Next Generation Learning, the Center for Curriculum Redesign, BELLXcel, Summit Learning, Teach to One, and countless others can point the way. Some of the nation's charter schools have taken a lead in developing new models of learning and innovative approaches to instruction, engaging students and families, and strategies for nurturing teaching talent.

Teaching will change dramatically with the advent of online tools and platforms. Teachers will need extensive professional development opportunities in order for them not only to transfer their curricula online, but, even if school is in person, to learn how to use the tools of technology to enhance instruction and extend learning opportunities to students in nonschool hours. Our schools are generally well behind the curve in adopting twenty-first-century tools for instructional purposes. Now is the time to surge forward.

Professional development will also be required for teachers to develop new curricula, applied learning opportunities, parent engagement strategies, personalized student success plans, and strategies for nurturing student relationships. New approaches to staffing and scheduling and a more flexible, nimble professional structure must be developed. This kind of professional learning will take time, and must be teacher led, designed by and for teachers, but drawing on the expertise of early adopters, experts, and tech leaders from other sectors. These changes in teacher role and practice are essential for any of these paradigm shifts to work, but in order for them to happen, schools must provide training and emphasize learning for the adults every bit as much as for the children.

It is time to envision significant shifts in how the delivery of education is organized. Once again, the current crisis creates a "necessity is the mother of invention" moment. With schools for the foreseeable future operating in limited and interrupted ways because of the Covid-19 threat, schools and entrepreneurs are already contemplating the modularization of education, offering new packages of content in new ways, contemplated by educators in different roles. Math education might come through one channel, while science education comes through another. One subcontractor might specialize in arranging virtual internships, while another might develop a set of online simulations. Organizations like City Year, with national service corps members, might supply talented, aspiring young educators to be the connective tissue between schools, teachers, and families, offering support on everything from technical internet connections to off-site tutoring. On the other hand, states might strengthen already promising efforts to offer statewide classes by some of the top teachers to be curated and supported locally by resident teachers and aides. Building on the experience of innovative online providers like Southern New Hampshire University and the Duet model, K–12 educators can begin to redesign a system for the future that will have value and endurance well beyond the current crisis.

To capitalize on the opportunities for change, our field will need to be nimble and adaptive, not qualities generally attributed to mainstream US public education. As always, we will need to keep our eye on equity. Affluent families have the financial resources and social capital to adapt in these challenging times by finding new ways and means of delivering learning to their children. For example, corona pods have lately been emerging in which a small number of families come together to hire their own teacher to provide customized instruction for their children. Obviously, all families cannot afford to do this. If we are not careful in this moment, we could devolve into being a Darwinian, "every man for himself" kind of education system in which education services become modularized and markets determine access to quality learning. Choice and innovative new options are promising prospects for education as long as they can be offered in ways that do not deepen already pernicious opportunity gaps.

In order to promote these kinds of transformational changes, we will need strong, enlightened leadership and a clear-eyed sense of the challenges ahead.

Leadership

We must have leaders with a special blend of traits and skills, including courage, social justice values, persistence, interpersonal skills, empathy, listening, imaginative vision, trust, and political acuity to move an agenda of change.

Vision

Leaders, in consultation with and the support of their communities, will bring clarity to the challenge of system redesign, seeing that poverty, race, and disadvantage matter and must be addressed; that schools alone are not enough to provide children with equal opportunity; that a new social compact is needed between communities and families; that society has paramount moral and economic imperatives to educate all children, and all means all, to high levels; that our ideals of excellence and equity are not being realized but could be if we created a system intentionally designed to achieve that equal opportunity society. Throughout the process of change, the vision must sustain the community's ideals of an excellent and equitable society that prepares all its children for work, citizenship, family life, lifelong learning, and personal fulfillment.

Strategy

To build an equal opportunity society that levels the playing field between those who enjoy the learning benefits of privilege and financial and social capital and those who don't is a monumental challenge and will require sweeping changes and highly effective strategy. Such a system resembles a cradle-to-career pipeline with highly functioning core component systems of early childhood, K–12, and postsecondary education. These subsystems must be full access and high quality. Wrapped around the core pipeline are complementary systems of support and opportunity that make it possible for each child to have what they need to show up to school each day throughout the K–12 years ready to learn and to take full advantage of an optimized schooling system. Strategy selection will be key to making all this happen.

Timing

Leaders will need to know what to do and when to do it. Leaders will understand when the opportunities for change present themselves and when people are too weary and traumatized to consider change. They will know that trust is essential to moving change; that change often means loss, shedding old ways; and that addressing the anxiety of embracing new ways and creating safety for those willing to do it is imperative. This is especially true in a time of crisis such as the present. Finally, leaders will know how to build their organizations' capacity to execute new strategies and work differently. Leaders will need to be gifted team builders, building on the expertise of their professional educators and sharing the work of leadership with their teams while providing them the time and support necessary to find new ways of working.

Challenges

To make any, let alone several, of these changes will require attention to an array of potential challenges and impediments.

Scarce, highly contested resources

Needs are urgent in all fields of government and human endeavor right now. The competition for scarce resources will be fierce, and the economy is likely to be struggling for some years to come. Taxpayers and policy makers will have agonizing decisions to make about budgets. While some believe that significant change is best precipitated in times of recession when organizations are forced to do more with less, others worry that the lack of financing for capacity building and program development will guarantee that recovery looks a lot like a restoration of the status quo. It will be impossible to generate the necessary resources to ensure equitable systems for all children to succeed without changes in tax policy. Philanthropies should not be funding basic services and supports in our society. Again, Children's Cabinets are well situated to lead the advocacy charge for more attention and resources to children's needs.

Focused attention, urgency

Like financing, public attention is a scarce and valued commodity. Urgent needs for rebuilding the economy; bringing back jobs; and attacking racism, police brutality, homelessness, food scarcity, criminal justice reform, and health care, to name a few, will compete for the public's attention with the redesign of our child development and education systems proposed in this book. Furthermore, we cannot have an effective education system if the population's basic human needs are unmet. Education should not be competing for funds with children's and families' health care or nutrition. However, human capital development systems, which are what our outdated school systems are, urgently need attention. We must recognize that building human capital is an essential long-term investment for which today's leaders must make a compelling case in order to focus the public's near-term attention on these needs. Leaders working together with Children's Cabinets can substantially increase the visibility and urgency of children's needs in their communities.

Adult interests

There is always some measure of both overlap and tension between the interests of children and the interests of adults when considering fundamental change in basic systems. Too often, adult interests triumph over children's interests in key educational decisions. At the same time, the biggest enemies of reform are complacency and the inertia of the status quo, the tendency of reform to be modestly incremental and complement existing structures, interests, and power relationships within existing systems. To overcome the resistance to change that arises from virtually all constituencies in the education and human development sector, leaders must create a compelling value proposition for working differently and a safe environment that allows people on the front lines to embrace change. For example, the kinds of paradigm shifts described above will require unprecedented levels of flexibility, imagination, and innovation from both management and labor unions in education.

Governance and accountability

Big shifts involving big changes in business as usual and significant investment of public resources will require oversight, reconsideration of governance mechanisms, and new tools for assessment and accountability. For example, it would be worth examining whether our existing structures for governing the work of educating and developing children are best suited to the kind of lifelong learning, holistic view of child development advanced in this book. To take the schooling system alone, saying nothing about all the child welfare agencies, our governance mechanisms are generally fragmented into early childhood, elementary and secondary, and higher-education silos. Wouldn't it make more sense to create an overarching governance system providing oversight and integration that is consistent and complementary across all levels? Or, wouldn't it be better, as suggested above, to have local Children's Cabinets in every community or region to coordinate policy, resources, and programs to optimize healthy child development and effective education?

At the level of service delivery, many of the proposed paradigm shifts would require new, different, more refined instruments of assessment and evaluation that would serve as the basis for a broader and deeper accountability system. In education, for example, there is a growing awareness of the need to nurture children's social and emotional development; to enhance their interpersonal skills, which are essential to workplace success; and to strengthen their relationships to teachers and mentors and their capacities to work in groups as they will in future jobs, yet we lack valid and reliable assessment tools to measure how schools are contributing to children's growth in these and other areas. To be sure, there is promising national work going on in organizations like CASEL and Partnerships in Education and Resilience (PEAR) on these topics, but the state of the art is early stage, and adoption of these tools is the exception rather than the rule. We continue to need ever more sophisticated tools for measuring students' academic progress, for both diagnostic and accountability purposes. However, to shift the paradigms, we'll need a much more robust system.

It will be especially challenging to develop evaluation tools to measure the value-added of our formal institutions of child development and education in terms beyond relatively simple measures of academic achievement. For example, what kinds of tools and protocols would be necessary to measure how and to what degree a particular school effectively cultivates strong working relationships with parents, high levels of student engagement, and successful student teamwork on applied learning projects? How do we determine whether each child has an effective adult mentor or counselor or whether student advisories are adding value? Ultimately, how do we do a much better job of determining the degree to which our schools are preparing our young people to be successful in college and career, allowing them to attain at least middle-class status by middle age? Assistance in the area of evaluation can found at Harvard's Center for Education Policy Research.

Policy, politics, equity, and public will

Many of the paradigm shifts proposed can be advanced in various ways by existing policies such as Medicaid or the Every Student Succeeds Act (ESSA). At the same time, changes in existing policies will also be required. For example, the return to school will necessitate significant shifts in ESSA policy about assessment and accountability. Some established policies make room, if thoroughly examined, for a number of the kinds of changes envisioned in this book, as do various state and local policies. Leaders at all levels commonly underutilize their own existing powers to make change because the resistance to change is often formidable and usually has political costs. New policies will be required to enact many of the contemplated paradigm shifts, and in order to engineer such policy changes, leaders will have to be thoughtful and strategic in crafting language and building coalitions to support the kind of sea changes that will bring our education and human development systems into the twenty-first century.

Children's Cabinets must courageously embrace the policy challenges presented by this equity work. While it is understandable and comfortable to shy away from potentially divisive political battles over policy, Cabinets must recognize that it will be difficult to move this children's work forward unless and until basic needs of children and families, like health care, nutrition, stable housing, and personal safety, are met. We must insist on progress in these domains as an absolute prerequisite of our work. Cabinets must take positions while simultaneously implementing solutions to meet immediate community needs. Cabinets must toggle between short- and long-term strategies for change, operating both simultaneously.

The Covid-19 crisis, coupled with the murder of George Floyd and its aftermath, have revealed profound and disturbing realities to the general public, creating a moment of opportunity for change and advancing equity. Genuine community leaders will know how to seize this opportunity to make change, whether it's as simple as guaranteeing, through policy changes, that every family has the education technology and internet access to make online learning an effective strategy for all or whether it's as complex as ensuring that all of our citizens, especially our children, have access to quality health care and nutrition.

All of these endeavors will require the building of public will. Organizing and listening to the public, parents, students, and community members—the presumed beneficiaries of the proposed paradigm shifts—will be an essential departure point. Incorporating their perspective in final policy products is imperative. People support what they help create. Children's Cabinets are ideal advocacy organizations for building public will in support of a bold children's agenda.

There are natural and deep constituencies for some of the proposed changes, while others will be met with stiff opposition. Not everyone agrees, for example, that schools have any business in developing children's social and emotional capacities, in spite of employers' insistence that these skills matter. Opponents will complain of government overreach. Others will fight for the interests of adults, privilege, race, jobs, money, and other prerogatives. Skillful leadership and widespread public demand can overcome such resistance, but not without deep strategic thought and organizing. The kinds of changes proposed here will only be successfully implemented if they are made top priorities rather than incidental things to accomplish. Adopting measures like these will require visionary leadership and deep community engagement through organizations like Children's Cabinets. We are confident that this can be done because we have seen successful examples of this kind of work in communities all across this country.

There are numerous thought-leading organizations in the policy and finance space. To name just a few: the Learning Policy Institute, Education Resource Strategies, the University of Washington's Center on Reinventing Public Education, the National Center on Education and the Economy, the Children's Funding Project, and Columbia University's Center for Educational Equity. One state that has taken the lead with some exemplary legislation is Maryland and its Blueprint for Maryland's Future.

CONCLUSION

We wish there were easy solutions to the challenges described above, but obviously there aren't. Meeting these challenges is the stuff of leadership. We believe Children's Cabinets are ideal mechanisms for providing the kinds of leadership the nation's challenges now demand. We desperately require action to envision, embrace, and enact a bold new agenda for preparing our young people to be successful in work, citizenship, and life. Children's Cabinets are catalysts for leadership action in both policy and implementation.

Each of the potential paradigm shifts described above will require monumental effort to enact. Any one of these changes would have substantial impact on young people's prospects for success. Taken together, any combination of multiple shifts has the potential to dramatically magnify the positive impact on children. Changes of this magnitude must be embraced by as many people as possible in a community. Again, Children's Cabinets are a mechanism for bringing people together to consider, shape, and embrace new directions.

To conceive of learning as lifelong; to bolster a neglected system of early education; to approach our children as unique individuals and customize education to meet their particular needs; to deepen learning by making it more engaging, and student- and project-centered; to intentionally cultivate and celebrate relationships between students and their teachers; to meaningfully engage families for the first time ever; and to embrace and capitalize on the tools of technology—all of these shifts, taken together, would revolutionize education and child development in the United States. These paradigm shifts would provide the foundation for migrating our outdated, outmoded system away from its early twentieth-century roots and into the bright light and new challenges of the twenty-first century.

Through it all, we must firmly fix our sights on building a system that is both excellent and, above all, equitable. We cannot do this without taking into account factors like poverty, racism, special needs, immigration, and the challenges of learning English. We can do far better than what we are doing now. This crisis gives our communities, and our Cabinets, an unprecedented opportunity to seize the moment and create a movement to redesign our strategies and structures for developing and educating our children. Now is the time to lead on policy and action. Let's not miss the opportunity and revert by defaulting to the status quo ante. Let's move forward! Together, we can.

APPENDIX

Map of Local Children's Cabinets in the United States

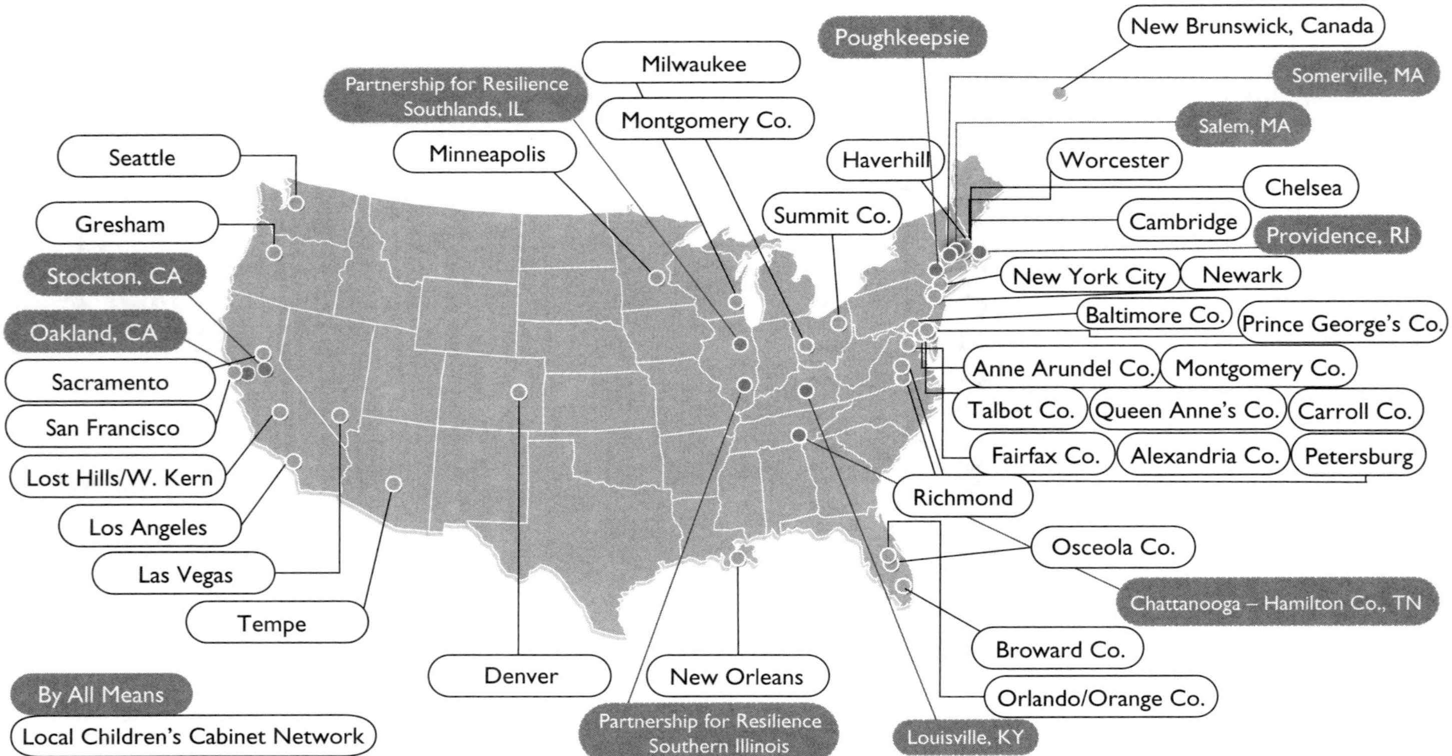

Seattle
Gresham
Stockton, CA
Oakland, CA
Sacramento
San Francisco
Lost Hills/W. Kern
Los Angeles
Las Vegas
Tempe
Partnership for Resilience Southlands, IL
Minneapolis
Milwaukee
Montgomery Co.
Denver
New Orleans
Partnership for Resilience Southern Illinois
Summit Co.
Haverhill
Poughkeepsie
New Brunswick, Canada
Somerville, MA
Salem, MA
Worcester
Chelsea
Cambridge
Providence, RI
New York City
Newark
Baltimore Co.
Prince George's Co.
Anne Arundel Co.
Montgomery Co.
Talbot Co.
Queen Anne's Co.
Carroll Co.
Fairfax Co.
Alexandria Co.
Petersburg
Richmond
Osceola Co.
Chattanooga – Hamilton Co., TN
Broward Co.
Orlando/Orange Co.
Louisville, KY
By All Means
Local Children's Cabinet Network

Notes

Preface

1. Rich Motoko et al., "Money, Race and Success: How Your School District Compares," *New York Times,* April 29, 2016, https://www.nytimes.com/interactive/2016/04/29/upshot/money-race-and-success-how-your-school-district-compares.html.
2. David B. Tyack and Larry Cuban, *Tinkering Toward Utopia: A century of public school reform* (Cambridge, MA: Harvard University Press, 1995).

Introduction

1. John Kania and Mark Kramer, "Collective Impact," *Stanford Social Innovation Review* 9, no. 1 (Winter 2011): 37–41.
2. Kania and Kramer, "Collective Impact."
3. C. J. Riehl et al., *Building Impact: A Closer Look at Local Cross-Sector Collaborations for Education* (New York: Teachers College, Columbia University, Department of Education Policy and Social Analysis, 2019).

Chapter 1

1. Benjamin R. Barber, *If Mayors Ruled the World: Dysfunctional Nations, Rising Cities* (New Haven, CT: Yale University Press, 2013), 4.
2. Proverbs 29:18 (King James Version).
3. The original cost of the scholarships was estimated at $125 to $150 million, but that number ballooned to around $500 million after more analysis. See Gaylen Moore et al., *Change at the Speed of Trust: Advancing Educational Opportunity Through Cross-Sector Collaboration in Louisville* (Cambridge, MA: Bloomberg-Harvard City Leadership Initiative, 2019).
4. Juan Sebastian Arias, *The People Behind the Movement: Mayor Greg Fischer,* (blog), Local and Regional Government Alliance on Race & Equity, September 8, 2017, https://www.racialequityalliance.org/2017/09/08/people-behind-movement-mayor-greg-fischer/.
5. Robert D. Putnam, *Our Kids: The American Dream in Crisis* (New York: Simon & Schuster, 2015).

6. John D. Donahue and Richard J. Zeckhauser, *Collaborative Governance: Private Roles for Public Goals in Turbulent Times* (Princeton, NJ: Princeton University Press, 2011), 263.

Chapter 2

1. John Kania and Mark Kramer, "Collective Impact," *Stanford Social Innovation Review* 9, no. 1 (Winter 2011): 37–41.
2. Elizabeth E. Gaines, Olivia Allen, and Amelia Vaughn, *A Children's Cabinet Toolkit: A Roadmap for Getting Started in Your Community* (Cambridge, MA: Education Redesign Lab, 2019).
3. See the website of 55,000 degrees: http://www.55000degrees.org/about-55k/.
4. Gaines et al., *A Children's Cabinet Toolkit,* 17–18.
5. See, for example, Tom Wolff, "Ten Places Where Collective Impact Gets It Wrong," *Stanford Social Innovation Review* (blog), May 4, 2016, https://independentsector.org/resource/voices-from-the-field-10-places-where-collective-impact-gets-it-wrong/.
6. Ronald Heifetz, *Leadership Without Easy Answers* (Cambridge, MA: Belknap Press of Harvard University Press, 1994).

Chapter 3

1. Michael McAfee, Angela Glover Blackwell, and Judith Bell, *Equity: The Soul of Collective Impact* (Oakland, CA: PolicyLink, 2015).
2. Anthony Iton and Robert Ross, "Understanding How Health Happens: Your Zip Code Is More Important Than Your Genetic Code," in *Public Health Leadership: Strategies for Innovation in Population Health and Social Determinants,* ed. Richard Callahan and Dru Bhattacharya (New York: Routledge, 2017).
3. Raj Chetty et al., "Where Is the Land of Opportunity? The Geography of Intergenerational Mobility in the United States," *Quarterly Journal of Economics* 129, no. 4 (November 2014): 1553–1623.
4. "Our Top Priority: Racial Equity," All Hands Raised, accessed October 30, 2020, https://allhandsraised.org/shared-work/top-priority.
5. "Educational Equity in Hamilton County," Chattanooga 2.0, accessed October 31, 2020.
6. Karen L. Mapp and Eyal Bergman, Dual Capacity-Building Framework for Family-School Partnership Version 2, 2019, at www.dualcapacity.org.
7. "Racism and inequity are products of design. They can be redesigned," Equity Design, https://medium.com/equity-design/racism-and-inequity-are-products-of-design-they-can-be-redesigned-12188363cc6a.
8. Courses.equitymeetsdesign.com.
9. "Targeted Universalism," Othering & Belonging Institute, accessed October 31, 2020.

Chapter 5

1. Lynne Sacks, Kenneth Wong, and Peter Deutscher, *Using Metrics to Sustain Collaborative Action for Children* (Cambridge, MA: Education Redesign Lab, 2020).

2. "Impact," Graduate Tacoma, accessed October 30, 2020, https://graduate tacoma.org/impact/ .
3. Additional resources on data sharing include: US Department of Education, "Data-Sharing Tool Kit for Communities: How to Leverage Community Relationships While Protecting Student Privacy" (Washington, DC, 2016); Milbrey McLaughlin and Rebecca A. London, *From Data to Action: A Community Approach to Improving Youth Outcomes*, Harvard Education Letter Impact Series (Cambridge, MA: Harvard Education Press, 2013).

Chapter 6

1. To see a more complete listing, see "Local Dedicated Children's Funds," Children's Funding Project, accessed October 30, 2020, https://www.childrens fundingproject.org/local-dedicated-funds?rq=local%20dedicated%20funds.

Chapter 7

1. Paul Reville, "Coronavirus Gives Us an Opportunity to Rethink K-12 Education," *Boston Globe,* April 9, 2020.
2. Elaine Weiss and Paul Reville, *Broader, Bolder, Better: How Schools and Communities Help Students Overcome the Disadvantages of Poverty* (Cambridge, MA: Harvard Education Press, 2019).

Acknowledgments

This book draws on the challenging and inspirational work of many people in the Harvard Education Redesign Lab's By All Means consortium and in many other communities who are building new, collaborative systems to more effectively educate and support children and youth. We thank all of these leaders, especially those in By All Means, for partnering with us and sharing their journeys with us over the past four years. We are inspired by what you have accomplished so far and look forward to continuing our joint efforts. We also thank Bridget Rodriguez for her dedicated and skillful leadership of the By All Means consortium and for her thoughtful input on the book.

A number of people contributed substantively to the material included here. Elizabeth Gaines, Olivia Allen, and Amelia Vaughn of the Children's Funding Project authored the toolkit that informs the Children's Cabinet chapter. They and Mary Ellen Wiggins of the Forum for Youth Investment all gave valuable input on that chapter, and their thinking and work over many years to support Children's Cabinets is reflected throughout the book. Other organizations such as Strive Together, the Collective Impact Forum, FSG, and the Tamarack Institute have all been foundational for developing a vision for the potential of cross-sector collaboration to improve entrenched social challenges. Eyal Bergman shaped our thinking about community and family engagement and has given valuable support on the topic to By All Means communities. Lyndsay Pinkus developed much of the Measures of Success framework and initial tools. Our colleague Jennifer Davis assisted us in our thinking about the future of early childhood education. We greatly appreciate all of their contributions. We are also very fortunate to have Nancy Walser as our editor at the Harvard Education Press. We thank her for her thoughtful input throughout this process.

We also thank all our wonderful colleagues at the EdRedesign for their hard work every day to make this vision a reality. Lynne would like to thank Paul for his decades of being a leading voice for addressing the most persistent challenges for children, his mentorship, and for being such a wonderful collaborator. Paul is so appreciative of Lynne's colleagueship, insights, and leadership not only in writing this book but in creating a successful EdRedesign, especially in its research and publications work, where she is a master. We also appreciate the support of the Harvard Graduate School of Education, particularly current dean Bridget Terry Long and former dean Jim Ryan, and our funders for EdRedesign's ongoing work. In particular, we thank the Linda Hammett Ory & Andy Ory Charitable Trust, Franklin W. Hobbs, the Carnegie Corporation of New York, the Oak Foundation, the Shah Family Foundation, the Schwartz Family Foundation, the Commonwealth Children's Fund, and the Nellie Mae Education Foundation for their generous support of our work.

Finally, we thank our respective families for their encouragement and patience through the process of writing the book. Paul is grateful to Julie for her patience and support on yet another project. Lynne thanks her husband, Paul, and children, Anna, Maya, and David, for their support, patience, and periodic distraction. Anna's help reviewing the final manuscript was especially valuable. Our children and grandchildren give us the inspiration to do and persist in this work.

About the Authors

Paul Reville is the Francis Keppel Professor of Practice of Educational Policy and Administration at the Harvard Graduate School of Education (HGSE), where he has been a faculty member since 1997. He is the founding director of HGSE's Education Redesign Lab. Reville served as secretary of education for the Commonwealth of Massachusetts from 2008 to 2013. His career, spanning more than four decades, has combined research, policy, and practice focused on educational equity and reform in Massachusetts and the nation. He has been a top policy maker, a teacher, a principal, and the founder of a research center and several other organizations devoted to education equity and reform.

During his service as the secretary of education for the Commonwealth of Massachusetts and as Governor Patrick's top education adviser, Reville established a new Executive Office of Education and had oversight of higher education, K–12, and early education in the nation's leading student achievement state. He served in the governor's cabinet and played a leading role on matters ranging from the Achievement Gap Act of 2010 and Common Core State Standards to the commonwealth's highly successful Race to the Top proposal. Before joining the Patrick administration, Reville had chaired the Massachusetts State Board of Education, founded the Rennie Center for Education Research and Policy, cofounded the Massachusetts Business Alliance for Education (MBAE), chaired the Massachusetts

Reform Review Commission, chaired the Massachusetts Commission on Time and Learning, and served as executive director of the Pew Forum on Standards-Based Reform, a national think tank that convened leading US researchers, practitioners, and policy makers to set the national standards agenda. Reville played a central role in MBAE's development of, and advocacy for, the Massachusetts historic Education Reform Act of 1993.

Reville began his career with service as a VISTA volunteer and youth worker. He worked as a teacher and principal of two urban alternative high schools. He founded a local education foundation, which was part of the Public Education Network, where he also served as a member of the national board. He has recently served as cochair of the national Broader, Bolder Approach to Education initiative. He is currently a board member of, and adviser to, a host of organizations such as City Year Boston, BELLXcel, Bellwether, Boston After School and Beyond, the Rennie Center, and Harvard Medical School's MEDscience program. He is a frequent writer, commentator, and speaker on education reform and policy issues. He holds a bachelor's degree from Colorado College, a master's degree from Stanford University, and five honorary doctorate degrees.

Additionally, Reville is the regular education commentator for WGBH's Boston Public Radio. He frequently contributes to *Education Week*, the *Boston Globe, The 74 Million*, and other publications. He has recently written for the *Times Education Supplement*, *Nature Human Behaviour*, and the publication of the Federal Reserve Bank of Boston. He co-edited the book *A Decade of Urban School Reform: Persistence and Progress in the Boston Public Schools*. He co-wrote, with Elaine Weiss, the book *Broader, Bolder, Better: How Schools and Communities Help Students Overcome the Disadvantages of Poverty*.

Lynne Sacks is the research director at the Education Redesign Lab and a lecturer at the Harvard Graduate School of Education. She leads EdRedesign's research activities, including the ongoing By All Means research as well as EdRedesign's other research, and teaches a graduate course on qualitative evaluation. Her publications include *Building Citywide Systems of Opportunity for Children*, *Sustaining Cross-Sector Systems of Opportunity for Children*, "Equity and Personalized Learning: A Research Review," and the *Stanford Social Innovation Review* article, "Sustaining Collaborative Action," which she coauthored with Paul Reville.

Before joining EdRedesign, Sacks worked for the Center for Equity and Excellence in Education at the George Washington University and the National Center on Education and the Economy on improving the school-to-work transition, benchmarking the US system against other countries, and improving programs for English learners. She has conducted research for the Massachusetts Department of Elementary and Secondary Education and the American Institutes for Research; she has also served as a consultant to New Profit, the Annenberg Center for School Reform, the Massachusetts Executive Office of Education, and the Commonwealth Corporation. A former English and English as a Second Language teacher, she earned her undergraduate degree from Cornell University and her MEd and EdD degrees from the Harvard Graduate School of Education.

Index